HUMAN RESOURCE ALIGNMENT

HUMAN RESOURCE ALIGNMENT

FROM BUSINESS STRATEGY TO HR PRACTICE

STEPHEN M FLYNN

Matador
9 Priory Business Park,
Wistow Road, Kibworth Beauchamp,
Leicestershire. LE8 0RX
Tel: 0116 279 2299
Email: books@troubador.co.uk
Web: www.troubador.co.uk/matador
Twitter: @matadorbooks

ISBN 978 1788033 695

British Library Cataloguing in Publication Data.
A catalogue record for this book is available from the British Library.

Printed and bound by CPI Group (UK) Ltd, Croydon, CR0 4YY

Typeset in 11pt Minion Pro by Troubador Publishing Ltd, Leicester, UK

Matador is an imprint of Troubador Publishing Ltd

Dedicated to the life force of Catherine Rachel Flynn, 1988–2006

CONTENTS

TABLES

ABBREVIATIONS

AOP	Annual Operating Plan
BJT	Basic Job Training
BSC	Balanced Scorecard
C&B	Compensation & Benefits
C&T	Calibre & Talent
CAP	Corrective Action Plan
CARDE	Calibre Acquisition, Retention, Development and Exit
CDE	Career Development Experience
CDT	Career Development Training
CEO	Chief Executive Officer
CFO	Chief Finance Officer
CI	Continuous Improvement
CoE	Centre of Excellence
COO	Chief Operating Officer
CoP	Community of Practice
CPD	Continuing Professional Development
CRAGS	Crimson, Red, Amber, Green, Silver colour-coding system
CRB	Calibre Review Board
DMU	Decision-Making Unit
EAP	Employee Assistance Programme
ED	Employee Development
EE	Employee Engagement
EM	Employee Motivation
EPM	Enterprise Performance Management system
ER	Employee Relations
ERP	Enterprise Resource Planning system
ESOP	Employee Share Ownership Plan
FYR	Full-Year Review
GM	General Manager
HIPO	High Potential
HPWS	High Performance Work System

HR	Human Resources
HRBP	Human Resources Business Partner
HRIS	Human Resource Information System
HRM	Human Resource Management
HRM	Human Resources Manager
HRML	Human Resource Maturity Level
HRMM	Human Resource Maturity Model
$HRMM_x$	Human Resource Maturity Matrix
HRSS	Human Resources Shared Service centre
IAR	Individual Accountability Review
ICP	Individual Career Plan
ICR	Individual Contribution Report
IDA	Individual Development Action
IDP	Individual Development Plan
JD	Job Description
KPI	Key Performance Indicator
KRA	Key Results Area
KSA/E	Knowledge, Skills, Abilities/Experience
LCD	Lowest Common Denominator
L&D	Learning and Development
LTIP	Long-Term Incentive Plan
MBE	Management By Exception
MbO	Management by Objectives
MBWA	Management By Walking About
MICAD	Management Information for Control and Decision-making
MIS	Management Information System
ML	Maturity Level
MoE	Measure of Effectiveness
MSOP	Minimum Standards of Performance
MYR	Mid-Year Review
OD	Organisational Design and Development
OE	Organisational Effectiveness
OJR	On-the-Job Reinforcement

OJT	On-the-Job Training
OML	Organisational Maturity Level
OSM	Office of Strategic Management
OTIF	On-Time, In-Full
PACER	Purpose, Agenda, Conduct, Expectations, Roles meeting planner
PADR	Performance And Development Review
PET	Performance Excellence Training
PDP	Personal Development Plan
PHI	Permanent Health Insurance
PIP	Performance Improvement Plan
PMI	Private Medical Insurance
PMO	Programme Management Office
PMS	Performance Management System(s)
R&R	Reward & Recognition
RCA	Root-Cause Analysis
RP	Recovery Plan
RRAA	Role, Responsibility, Authority and Accountability
RTW	Return To Work
SBU	Strategic Business Unit
SIB	Sales Incentive Bonus
SIP	Sales Incentive Plan
SKPI	Strategic Key Performance Indicator
SLA	Service Level Agreement
SMART	Specific, Measurable, Achievable, Relevant and Time-trackable
SME	Subject Matter Expert
SMT	Self-Managed Team
SOFI	Statement Of Future Intent
SOFP	Sales Order Fulfillment Process
SOI	Statement Of Intent
SOP	Standard Operating Procedure
SP	Specific Proposal
SPOC	Single Point Of Contact

STIP	Short-Term Incentive Plan
T&A	Time & Attendance system
T&C	Terms & Conditions
TM	Talent Management
TNA	Training Needs Analysis
TQM	Total Quality Management
VP	Vice President
VSM	Viable Systems Model
VTT	Variance To Target
WBAWI?	What Business Are We In?

PREFACE

For some 35 years or more, I have been grappling with the people issues and problems that arise in large organisations. For over 20 years, I have been tasked with defining and deploying the human resource strategies for six diverse organisations. In all that time, I have had the pragmatic challenge of tailoring such strategies to fit the context of each business. Throughout, I have, like many HR professionals, struggled with the contrast and conflict between corporate 'strategy', HR 'strategy' and HR 'operational practice'. To put it another way, I had to work out how to 'translate' from corporate strategy all the way through to HR practice.

Over these years, I have been fortunate enough to have worked for some very tolerant employers. They have allowed me to 'experiment' on their enterprises and work through the challenges mentioned above. Each business had its own unique issues and was at a distinct stage of development. Fortunately, each business sought an HR contribution to 'fix' its problems. It is through this very real 'action research' that I have been able to compose this book. From the solutions that we crafted for the different businesses, and from the reviews of what worked and what did not, a generic model eventually emerged. This practical model arose from the real needs of the business; it was not derived from theory. That model is captured in this book.

The model we describe in this book is, in essence, still a live experiment – a form of action learning that has been tested across some 25 organisations. It continues to evolve as it is tested in new contexts. This is the third edition that explains that model, the HR Maturity Model (HRMM). This volume was first published under the title 'Linking Human Resource Strategy and Practice', then under the title 'Human Resource Maturity Matrix'. This book is a complete rewrite of the earlier editions. The model has been fine-tuned and new material has been added. However, the research and the work go on. In fact, the reader is invited to test this model in their own context. By following the methodology in this book, they will be able to add to the body of knowledge.

This book is not just my thought and deeds. It is the accumulated experience and ideas of a host of line managers, directors, vice presidents,

CEOs, HR specialists and employees who have participated in the action research, knowingly or unknowingly. The HR plans and practices set out in this book are the product of some excellent HR teams that I have had the privilege to be a part of and, in some cases, the honour to have led. In fact, the final model discussed in this book arose from several series of workshops stretching over a number of years. Thus, I have merely captured the thoughts, actions and insights of those teams and businesses in what I hope is a concise and coherent manner. However, all errors remain my own.

The approach in this book is both deductive and inductive. At first, my teams and I drew on our professional experiences. We identified which HR practices worked – when and where. We noted those practices that did not work – when and where. We gradually fitted these jigsaw pieces together in a logical pattern. This pattern became the framework of the HRMM. We then positioned all the HR practices known to us in what came to resemble an HR version of the periodic table. It all seemed to fit. However, there were still some gaps. It was as if there were missing HR 'chemical elements' in our 'periodic table'. We then switched to an inductive approach. We followed the logic of the HRMM and speculated as to what HR practices could fill those gaps. Later experimentation proved that these practices did 'fit' both the organisational context and into the HRMM. Bit by bit, we filled the HRMM with HR practices that aligned with organisations at all levels of maturity.

It is impossible to name all those who have directly and indirectly contributed to this final work. However, I would like to acknowledge the contribution of a few close colleagues who helped me to break through the 'cloud of unknowing' to write this book: Sarah Hammond, Clare Porciani, Louise O'Brien, Sarah Kay, Helen Percival, Lisa Melling and Anne Griffiths.

Finally, I would like to thank my family, Anne and Dominic, for their patience and tolerance. Their unconditional love and devotion spurred me on. Lastly, my eternal acknowledgement goes to my intellectual inspiration, Catherine, a much-missed and much-loved scholar and daughter.

CHAPTER 1

INTRODUCTION

Solving the Conundrums of HRM

In this chapter, we will describe the fundamental problem for Human Resource Management in setting out its stall – defining the HR strategy, and selecting and implementing suitable HR practices to enact that strategy. We will explore the concepts of external and internal fit, as described in the professional literature. We will then describe the problems in locating and defining corporate strategy. We will discuss how this presents an almost insurmountable barrier to resolving HR's fundamental problem and see that there is the problem of a veritable 'Tower of Babel' at the heart of this conundrum. Business and HR strategy and practices occupy different domains and use different languages. We therefore reframe the problem and introduce a new tool to resolve the multiple dilemmas faced by HR policymakers and practitioners. We introduce the Human Resource Maturity Model (HRMM).

Scoping the HRM Problem

As we have already stated, the solution we offer in this book is the HRMM. So, to be clear, we should state what we see as the problem. Put simply, it is the perennial issue for the HR profession – relevance, alignment and added value. That is, relevance to the client organisation, alignment with the strategy of that organisation and proving how HR adds value to that business through the practices HR enacts. In the literature, these requirements have been labelled external and internal fit.

External Fit

In order for the business to survive, grow and prosper, it needs to align with the market. This is the top-level condition of external fit. As no market is static, this is a dynamic requirement. The enterprise must be agile to adjust to the shifts and discontinuities in and around its chosen markets.

More specifically for our purposes, the HR strategy must align with the strategy of the client firm. This is the second condition of external fit. A subset of this condition is the need to align with HR's own external environment – primarily, this is the labour market. We will simply note this subset at this stage as we have written in depth on this form of alignment in a companion volume and space does not permit the repetition of the arguments.

The literature implies that if HR is aligned – in other words, external fit is achieved – HR will, by definition, 'be strategic'. However, HR is frequently accused of *not* being strategic. Bogged down in transactional administrative activities, the profession is censured for its focus on the operational. HR does not speak 'business', but some foreign language. At best, much is lost in translation.

So, HR must firstly locate business strategy and then translate it. It is incumbent upon HR to do this, as the profession cannot expect the wider business to do it for them. We will return to the issue of external fit later in this chapter.

Internal Fit

There are two vectors here, which we will deal with in turn: vertical and horizontal.

Internal vertical fit is the alignment *within* the HR strategy itself. HR practices should follow from the HR strategy and all practices should be consistent with that strategy.

Here, we face a variation on the problem we discussed under external fit. Practices are expressed in concrete terms, whereas strategy is expressed in conceptual terms. Again, we have two different languages. Internal vertical fit is thus problematic.

When we turn to internal horizontal fit, things are no better. This subset of fit requires that alignment *across* HR specialisms is maintained at both the strategic and operational levels. So, the training strategy should match the C&B strategy and, for instance, the e-learning practices should align with the salary practices. All should be complementary.

Yet, as every HR professional knows, each specialism within HR speaks its own language. It is as if we face a veritable 'Tower of Babel'. There is a need for a universal translator! We will return to this need later in this chapter.

Locating Business Strategy

Let us now return to the challenge of alignment with the strategy of the enterprise – the requirement for so-called external fit. If we are to locate strategy, we need to know it when we see it. So, what does the literature say a 'good' strategy should consist of? There are many models to choose from, but we will take one in order to illustrate the issues facing HR. According to Hambrick and Fredrickson, a good business strategy consists of:

- Arenas
- Vehicles
- Differentiators
- Staging
- Economic logic.

Arenas define where the business will be active. It answers the question: what business are we in (WBAWI)? The answer should be as specific as possible in terms of product categories, market segments, geographical areas and core technologies. In addition, the firm needs to define which stages of the value-adding chain it will occupy and which it may outsource – from design through to distribution.

Vehicles specify the means by which the firm will enter the arenas. This can be through joint ventures, franchises, acquisitions, licensing or by developments internal to the firm.

Differentiators are the methods by which the business distinguishes itself from its competitors. This may be through image, customisation, price, style, reliability etc.

Rarely can all of the above be achieved in one go. Hence, *staging* is the plan of what to do, where and when. It is the execution and roll-out plan for the arenas, vehicles and differentiators. Some foundational work may have to be done first before grander schemes may be implemented effectively.

Finally, the strategy must make clear how profits will be generated. There needs to be a clear *economic logic* underpinning the other elements of the strategy. This may, for instance, be premium pricing for superior quality products or repeat business arising from exceptional customer service.

The above criteria for a 'good' strategy are demanding for any business. We would suggest that few businesses match up to this exacting standard.

Further, even if a firm met all of these criteria, there is no hint how this could be readily translated into HR terms. Yet, the problem is even deeper than this.

Strategy comes in many different guises. It is polysemic – that is, the word has multiple meanings. According to Mintzberg, strategy can be defined as:

- Perspective
- Position
- Plan
- Pattern
- Ploy.

Perspective is the shared concept that the organisation holds of itself. It is the enterprise's driving force, character or collective mind. A *position* is a niche or location in a given environment. A *plan* is a deliberate, conscious intention described in a series of logical steps. *Pattern* is an identifiable consistency in behaviour or stream of actions, whether this was consciously intended or not. Finally, a *ploy* is a specific manoeuvre to outwit a competitor.

So, we could suggest that an ideal strategy would be: clearly defined; comprehensive; translatable into the specialist functions within a business, so integrating all those functions into the overall strategy; and describing how long-term success will be attained. Then, such a business strategy could be readily translated into HR, and the HR plans could be devised, which, in turn, could be integrated back into the overall strategy.

Reality is, however, not that straightforward. Strategies are often unclear or even unstated. They are partial or incomplete. They rarely translate easily into all of the specialist functions. They may even be disconnected from some or all of those functions. Finally, the strategy may be relatively short-term. Alternatively, it may be timeless and captured in a mission statement. As Mintzberg has pointed out, the strategy may not be *deliberate*, but could be *emergent* – an evolving pattern, rather than a detailed plan.

Thus, locating strategy proves to be highly problematic. However, if we cannot locate strategy, we certainly cannot translate it. To resolve the need for external and internal fit, we need to take a different tack.

Deconstructing the Problem: Strategy versus Practice

As we have seen so far in this chapter, approaching the problem of alignment or fit head on does not get us very far. Let us explain why this is by way of an analogy – the 'climate change paradox'.

There is a strong body of evidence and opinion that we, as a planet, face the problem of global warming. Yet, in the UK, 2009/10 was the coldest winter in 30 years – statistically, that is a 1-in-20-year event. Then, 2010/11 was another cold winter – another 1-in-20-year event! So, without going into the science, how could we explain this apparent contradiction?

You cannot see climate, you can only see weather. Climate is a 'pattern of weather'. Similarly, you cannot see strategy, only practices. Strategy is to climate as practice is to weather. We have to infer climate from the pattern of weather. We have to infer strategy from patterns of work practices.

Diagnosing Strategy

Even if an organisation does not have a deliberate, well-articulated strategy, it does have practices – a firm *does* things. According to the Viable Systems Model (VSM), the purpose of a system or organisation is what it *does*. So, moving on from our climate analogy, if we can identify the pattern of work practices in an organisation, we may be able to infer the implied organisational strategy. Similarly, if we can identify the pattern of HR practices, we can infer the implied HR strategy.

Therefore, the problem of alignment or external fit is reduced to identifying the current pattern of work practices and matching it with a complementary pattern of HR practices.

Reframing the Problem

So, if the HR strategy is a pattern of HR practices, the challenge becomes:

- Which HR practices fit the organisation's pattern of work practices?
  - This gives external fit.
- Which practices across the HR specialisms are mutually complementary?
  - This gives internal horizontal fit.
- Which HR practices are unnecessary luxuries and when?
  - These would be strategic misfits.
- Given the organisational context, which HR practices do we develop and implement next?
  - This gives the HR plans.
- What is the underlying logic of the resultant pattern?
  - This defines the HR strategy and gives internal vertical fit.

All of the above questions can be answered using the HRMM.

Human Resource Maturity Model

The HRMM is a pattern of HR practices. It is a generic framework that:

- links HR strategy and HR practices
- is applicable to and aligns with all stages of organisational development
- is applicable to all organisations and sectors
- connects HR strategy with the (implicit) organisational strategy.

It is both a diagnostic tool and a framework for planning HR actions. It is the universal translator. The lingua franca is *maturity*.

Throughout this book, we will build up the HR Maturity Matrix (HRMM$_x$). The outline of the HRMM$_x$ is set out in Table 1. Space will not permit us to type all of the content into this outline. However, the complete HRMM$_x$ can be fitted onto one sheet of A4 paper – thus becoming 'a plan on a page'. This book will explain each cell of the HRMM$_x$, and how the content and positioning is complementary.

Table 1: Human Resource Maturity Matrix							
OML	HRML	OE	C&T	PMS	EE	ED	R&R

As a footnote, it is worth pointing out that the HRMM$_x$ is, in essence, a roadmap. It is a summary of the HRMM. However, the map is not the territory. By definition, a map is a simplified representation of the territory. Yet, it is a very useful guide to navigation across that territory.

Structure of the Book

Chapter 2

In this chapter, we define the purpose, nature and properties of maturity models in general and of the HRMM in particular. We then scope out the four maturity levels in the model we offer in this book. Firstly, we cover the four organisational maturity levels (OML) from entrepreneurial management to systematic management. We describe how the characteristics of the business evolve as a firm progresses through each maturity level. We show how each maturity level is a plateau on a continuous-improvement journey. We then set out the institutionalisation practices that ensure that new work practices are embedded in the organisation.

Secondly, we describe each HR maturity level that matches each OML. These are explained briefly here, as the details are reserved for later chapters. The OML forms the first axis of the $HRMM_x$.

Chapter 3
In this chapter, we set out a definition of the core purpose of Human Resources. This is then disaggregated into the six constituent pillars of the HR strategic framework, e.g. reward & recognition (R&R). Each pillar is given its own distinct definition. It is these pillars that form the second axis of the $HRMM_x$.

Chapters 4-9
In these chapters, we describe the detailed HR practices and themes that relate to each of the four maturity levels for each of the six pillars of the HR strategic framework. A step-change progression in the sophistication of these practices will be apparent as an organisation shifts from one maturity level to the next.

Chapter 10
Drawing on the previous six chapters, we present an overall model of employee motivation. We show how certain motivations are available and are facilitated by each maturity level, and those which remain inaccessible and under-developed at each ML. We show that employee motivation is a dependent variable – that is, dependent upon the OML. We therefore demonstrate the scope for, and the limitations of, 'psychological contracts' at each ML.

Chapter 11
In this chapter, we pull all of the HRMM together and demonstrate how to use it as a strategic diagnostic and planning tool. We explain the need to conduct a gap analysis and to focus the reader on matching and pacing the client organisation's maturity level. We then show how the $HRMM_x$ can be used to devise a 'plan on a page'.

Finally, we discuss how to market the resultant HR plan and to what extent an overt approach to internal marketing fits the context of the firm as defined by its OML or not.

Chapter 12

Here we explain the HR operating model in terms of dominant themes, workload, skills required, style, structure and role. We show how all these dimensions of the operating model change radically as an organisation, and especially that firm's HR function, step through the four maturity levels. We then reflect how this perspective affects the classic Ulrich model. We show that this classic model can only be progressively implemented in line with the maturity levels. We then present a qualified Ulrich model that fits with the logic and strictures of the HR maturity model. In short, we will show that, as far as any HR operating model is concerned, one size does not fit all.

Chapter 13

In this final chapter, we draw together all the threads running throughout the book. We scope the enormity of the task facing an organisation that may wish to follow the journey from maturity levels one to four. We then return to the debate between best practice and best fit. We show that this is a dichotomy as both are embedded in the HRMM. We explain that the description of each OML is in effect a surrogate for an explicit enterprise strategy and that the desire of HR to align with such a strategy is resolved by using the HRMM. Only at the most sophisticated maturity level (level four) is alignment to an *explicit* corporate strategy actually feasible. In other words, the holy grail of strategic alignment is a special case reserved for maturity level four.

We conclude by describing an holistic framework of HR strategy by revisiting Mintzberg's 5 Ps of strategy – perspective, position, plan, pattern and ploy.

Throughout this book we will use the terms 'organisation', 'firm', 'enterprise' and 'business' as interchangeable. We maintain that the HRMM is applicable to organisations in the public as well as the private sector. In addition, we will use references to the male and female gender, e.g. he or she, interchangeably. All such references are meant to refer to all genders.

How to Use this Book

This is not an academic book, although it is informed by good theory. Further, it is not a manual of tools and techniques. This is a short guidebook to aid the navigation of Human Resource strategy and the choice and deployment of HR practices. It derives from the experience of a host of practitioners who have tested these practices in real situations. As this is a guidebook, references are kept to a bare minimum, to aid ease of reading. Only where there is a direct or near quote does the reference appear in the body text. For more general references, the reader should go to the relevant section at the back of the book.

An understanding of the broad range of HR techniques is assumed. Readers are referred to the standard business school and professional development textbooks for an explanation of the mainstream tools mentioned in this volume. However, where a practice is offered that is not readily available in such textbooks, it is described more fully.

This book may be used in a number of ways. Firstly, it may be taken as merely a descriptive text. Here it sets out the patterns of practices that a number of HR practitioners discovered as they tried to resolve the problems in a varied set of organisations. Secondly, it may be used to diagnose the current state of both the client enterprise in general and that of its HR function in particular. Alignment or misalignment may thus be discovered. Thirdly, having done this, it could be used to conduct a gap analysis to see if that HR function was 'in sync' with its host business. Fourthly, given all this, this book can be used to craft relevant and congruent HR strategies, plans and practices that are aligned, consistent and coherent.

This book may be suitable firstly for senior HR practitioners who seek a strategic navigation aid. Secondly, in a similar vein, it may meet the needs of CEOs and COOs. Thirdly, it may be of interest to academics and students of HRM as a case study or as a basis for further study and research.

Summary

In this chapter we have scoped the HR problem as one of external and internal fit. That is, alignment of the HR strategy with the corporate strategy and internal consistency between all the HR practices. We have seen that this aim is fraught with problems; not least of these is actually locating corporate strategy. We showed that the test of any organisational strategy worthy of the name is so high that HR is set up for failure in achieving external and internal fit. We argued that taking this issue head on leads nowhere. Hence, we reframed the problem. We recognised that strategy and practice occupy different universes and are expressed in different languages. However, while strategy may be elusive and even unarticulated, practices are always present. The purpose of an organisation is what it does. We introduced the HRMM as a framework of work practices and HR practices that can distil the underlying purpose of any and all organisations. We also contended that the HRMM offers an effective and efficient solution to achieving external and internal fit. The rest of the book aims to prove this point in detail.

CHAPTER 2

ORGANISATIONAL AND HUMAN RESOURCE MATURITY

Introduction

In this chapter we will set out the first axis of the $HRMM_x$ – that of maturity levels themselves. We will explain the nature of maturity models in general, before covering the HRMM in particular. We will describe the organisational maturity levels in some detail. Each organisational maturity level (OML) has a unique collection of work practices that sets the context for all HR practices. We then explore the general properties of maturity models. It will be apparent that these properties both prescribe and proscribe actions and practices. We will then turn to the critical importance of embedding work practices in organisations through the so-called 'institutionalisation practices'. Finally, we introduce human resource maturity levels (HRML), one for each of the organisational maturity levels. The detailed HR practices for each HRML will be described in later chapters.

Maturity Models

Maturity models were devised due to the problems that arose when practitioners attempted to apply programmes such as Total Quality Management (TQM), software development etc. They realised that implementation had to progress in precise and structured stages. It became apparent that there was a series of ever-more sophisticated practices that needed to be put in place and in a set order.

Each work practice had to pass through an adoption curve of its own, through stages of: awareness; learning; piloting; deployment; and mastery (Curtis et al, p.7-8). Thus, there was an organisational learning curve to be followed to enhance the chances of successful implementation of the desired work practice. In essence, practitioners realised that 'best practice' (however defined) could not be achieved in one go, but involved the implementation of a series of applications of ever-increasing sophistication.

A maturity model is defined as a systematic methodology for raising the capability of work practices in a specific domain. A maturity model describes a journey from a collection of ad hoc practices to an integrated infrastructure of highly advanced practices. The model designates a staged roadmap, where each stage is a maturity level: "a stage of capability that is an evolutionary *plateau* on an organisational improvement path" (Curtis et al, 2002, p.512 – italics added). These levels are cumulative in that each level acts as a foundation for the next higher level. However, the improvement path is not a steady, monotonous, smooth gradient; the move between one ML to the next higher is a step-change discontinuity. The features of a maturity model will become apparent as we describe each ML in turn.

Organisational Maturity Levels

The number of maturity levels (ML) differs from model to model. In the HR domain, Curtis et al describe five, while Kearns defines seven. For our purposes, experience to date suggests that there is a core set of four, with some variations within two of these. As far as the OML we describe in this book are concerned, the levels are as follows:

1. Entrepreneurial Management
    a. Start-up
    b. Emerging
2. Process Management
    a. Unit level
    b. Organisation-wide
3. Proficiency Management
4. Systematic Management.

NB: For brevity, we will follow the convention of using the levels and numbers as follows from here on in: ML1, OML2a etc.

The descriptions of each ML have common headings or characteristics, but the actual content is radically distinct, reflecting the step-change differences between the various ML. The actual headings are set out in Table 2.

Most of these headings will be self-explanatory. So, we will only comment on the less obvious characteristics.

Table 2. Organisational Maturity Levels – Characteristics
Organisational focus
Measures of effectiveness
Nature of organisational 'strategy'
Open or closed system
The nature of work practices
The nature of project management
Organisational structure
Job design
Predominant management style
Predominant decision making style
Organisational climate

The organisational focus is the prime motivation at that stage of maturity which drives most activity in the enterprise. For instance, this may be survival or continuous improvement. It is implicit, rather than overt and articulated.

Open versus closed system refers to systems theory and describes how the firm relates to its environment. That is, whether it acts as if it were open to its environment or not, as demonstrated by its implicit focus and explicit actions.

Organisational structure is, in general, self-evident. However, for our purposes it is specifically the means of focussing management attention. Management attention is a scarce resource (Goold and Campbell, p.33) and "different structures direct management attention to different issues" (p.31). Hence, the structure follows from the organisational focus and the nature of 'strategy' associated with the specific organisational maturity level.

Actual management style will be very personal to each manager. However, each ML tends to attract and encourage certain styles while discouraging others. Hence, under each ML, there will tend to be a predominant style that prevails. The model we have adopted is the HAY Group Inventory of Management Styles, which consists of six styles: directive, visionary, affiliative, participative, pacesetting and coaching.

Finally, organisational climate is the recurring pattern of behaviours typical of a firm at that stage of maturity. It tends to be more accessible than organisational culture, although the two terms could be considered interchangeable for our purposes.

We will now describe the characteristics of organisations at each ML.

OMLIa – Entrepreneurial Management: Start-up

The focus of the firm is to launch and survive. The founder and her initial team want to get the bright idea or concept off the ground and into the market. Energy is concentrated on 'make and sell'. As a consequence, the measures of effectiveness (often implicit) are the rate of new product creation, creative solutions and growth.

The strategy is exploratory. Until the new concept hits the market, it is just that – a concept. Thus, there is no explicit strategy as such, as it is implicit. The priority is not on drafting a long-term strategic plan, but on securing immediate outcomes. This is not to say that a vision is lacking. Far from it, the founder could have a well-articulated vision that may attract and inspire her employees. This vision, though, has yet to be fully tested in its environment.

As a system, the organisation is very open. In fact, it may be too open. Almost all elements of the new firm are exposed to the market. Functions and activities that in later stages of maturity will be wholly internally-oriented will, at ML1a, be wide open to the environment.

There are no standard work practices or processes. A trial-and-error approach is evident. In effect, standardisation and codification would be premature at this stage. The employees have yet to work out the 'one best way' of doing anything. As the founding concept is tested, work practices evolve to meet the immediate demands and requirements of customers.

The organisational structure is fluid, to say the least. All coordination is done by and through the founder. Control is via direct interaction. This is feasible as the numbers of employees in the firm tend to remain small at ML1a.

In line with the lack of standard work practices, jobs are dynamic. Everyone 'mucks in' and 'muddles through', fulfilling what needs to be done on a daily, if not hourly, basis. Hence, there is no systematic job design as such, or at least not that would be recognised in any HR textbook.

The management style is a direct derivative of the personality of the founder. It will have elements of the visionary, naturally, at this stage of development. It may even be idiosyncratic. The founder may have a model

Table 3. Archetypal Start-up Employment Models			
Blueprint	*Attachment*	*Selection*	*Control*
'Star'	Interesting and challenging work	Long-term potential	Professional control
'Engineering'	Interesting and challenging work	Skills and experience to achieve the immediate tasks	Informal control by peers (culture)
'Commitment'	Family feeling and emotional bond to the firm	Values and cultural fit	Informal control by peers (culture)
'Bureaucracy'	Interesting and challenging work	Skills and experience to achieve the immediate tasks	Formal procedures and systems
'Autocracy'	Money	Skills and experience to achieve the immediate tasks	Direct oversight

that he explicitly or implicitly works to, perhaps in line with, or in opposition to, his experience of work and business to date.

Research suggests that the management style (and other characteristics of the start-up) falls into one of five archetypes – employment blueprints (see Baron and Hannan, 1999 and 2002). These are summarised in Table 3. These models differ along three dimensions: attachment and retention; criteria for employee selection; and means of control and coordination. *Attachment* is the nature of the bond between enterprise and employee. *Selection* refers to the predominant method of selecting and holding onto employees. *Control* refers to the primary methods of coordinating work. Even though these are referred to as blueprints, the models remain implicit and subliminal.

Decision-making is predominantly by gut-feel. This does not mean that the employees and founder do not draw on their own technical expertise. However, in a business sense, there is little data and few management tools yet installed in the enterprise. Further, there is limited time to deliberate in this context.

In common with the management style, the organisational climate is a derivative of the founder's persona. This is inculcated by direct contact with the founder for all employees.

OML1b – Entrepreneurial Management: Emerging

The firm has survived the start-up phase. The focus now shifts to consolidating market position and growing.

Through the trial and error of ML1a, the enterprise has found its niche and now it aims to exploit that niche. However, this strategy is still implicit. The organisation only formalises its strategy if required to do so by an external party, e.g. if seeking a loan from a bank or if acquired by venture capitalists. However, even if it does so, the document has limited influence on the actual running of the firm. Hence, any explicit strategy at this ML is a 'fantasy document'. In fact, any 'strategy' below ML3 is likely to be a 'duck': "… strategies that function as symbols, not roadmaps" (Liedtka, 2006, p.32). Such strategy 'ducks' offer little if any guidance to managers and employees on how to conduct business and thus may engender indifference, cynicism, fatigue and inertia in employees: "… symbolic strategies may well be worse than no strategy at all" (p.32).

The company as a system is moderately open in nature. The firm has grown to such a size that some roles are focused internally, with limited exposure to the outside world.

Work practices are now evolving. Workers have found optimal ways of getting the goods out of the door and so tend to comply with this rote methodology. The basic business processes work, in a fashion. However, they are erratic and subject to wide variation in performance. They go in and out of control – that is, they oscillate. There may be an enterprise resource planning system (ERP), but, due to poor process design and discipline, this does not control such volatility.

Despite the work becoming slightly standardised, there is limited codification of work practices. Under certain jurisdictions, such systematisation may be required by law, so the organisation may codify work practices, in a fashion. This reflects the tendency at ML1b towards compliance, both externally and internally. The prime internal control, however, is a basic financial system at this maturity level.

Project management is ad hoc. There is no methodology, as such. Attempts are made to deal with the process oscillations mentioned above, so projects do arise. However, there is no consistency of approach.

The organisation at this stage is evolving. As the size of the company grows, it becomes increasingly difficult for the founder to manage all the workers directly. The challenges of coordination increase with the number of employees at an exponential rate. The strain becomes too great for one person. Hence, she starts to hire managers on an ad hoc basis to fill the gaps as she sees them. Coordination is now via the founder and these new managers. However, there is no organising principle guiding a structural design per se. The structure that evolves may be archaic or even inherited if any takeover occurs. Managers may work by their own implicit or explicit 'folk model' of structure and style.

Consistent with the description so far, job design is ad hoc and ambiguous. Employees still get on with it as they did in ML1a, but with much less assurance as to whether they are doing the right thing.

At this level of maturity, outcomes are achieved almost exclusively by heroic effort (Curtis et al, p.8-9). Hence, the predominant management style is, just that, heroic. However, this in itself is not a consistent style. Due to the oscillations in the system, managers may be relatively laid-back some days, but in a directive mode other days. This generally confuses employees, who consequently keep their heads down and do what they have to do in order to get by.

Decision-making is still gut-feel as data is still scarce and when crises hit (which, at ML1b, they do frequently), there is no time to analyse the situation. Heroism is thus needed and encouraged.

The common climate, apparent at ML1a, now fragments. The atmosphere may well be fearful. So, a compliance culture emerges. As there are few guidelines and as initiative is not rewarded (except for the few 'heroes'), an air of 'irresponsible autonomy' is apparent. People get by and get away with what they can. The resolution of this crisis in the organisation's evolution is ML2.

OML2a – Process Management: Unit Level

The enterprise takes a quantum leap from ML1a to this level and the focus shifts to efficiency and stability, with the emphasis on the latter. Internal control is the order of the day. The executive management of the business commits to a set of policies over work practices and devotes the resources necessary to support practices that can enact such policies. Managers are held accountable for aligning work practices with the declared policies. However, each local unit is free to choose *how* the policies are implemented within their own unit. Through designing and applying such systematic practices, managers and employees learn how this approach helps to solve their immediate problems. This learning is essential to enable the firm to progress later to ML2b and beyond.

Consequently, measures of effectiveness at ML2a are efficiency of operation, timeliness, consistency and reliability.

There is still no explicit strategy at ML2a. Activity is very task-focused and the pattern that emerges suggests that the implied strategy is very operational in nature. Consistent with this, the organisation acts as if it were a closed system. The outside world intrudes only at the periphery. Most managers and employees are inwardly oriented.

A key characteristic of this stage of development is the Standard Operating Procedure (SOP). Virtually all business processes are codified, particularly in the operating core of the organisation, e.g. the Sales Order Fulfillment Process (SOFP). Business processes are mapped, in a basic sense, and the functional steps are captured in the SOP. In addition, there is a change-control process to ensure that SOPs remain robust and up-to-date.

An array of policy and procedure manuals thus emerge at this ML. These tend to contain some or all of the following: policy statements, procedural steps, management guidelines, authority levels, and documentation in hard or soft copy forms.

To support the change process, basic project management is apparent. Projects are, however, treated as isolated schemes. Yet a systematic methodology is followed at this ML, unique to each unit. Projects arise as needed, where improved efficiency is identified as desirable and obtainable.

There is now a clear organising principle that guides the design of the organisational structure. A formal functional structure is in place. This is the uniform structure or so-called U-form. To support this and to aid coordination, competent management teams emerge as a key tool and process. Formal coordination, however, rests on the shoulders of the General Manager in charge of the firm. We will, in the main, refer to this role as the Chief Executive Officer (CEO). Control and evaluation is through budgets and SOPs – again, in the main.

Job design is now also a formal process with its own SOP. Jobs tend to be defined quite narrowly. Thus, job specialisation is high, both horizontally and vertically. Horizontal specialisation describes the number of tasks a job covers. Vertical specialisation covers the degree of control a worker has over those tasks. So, at ML2, restrictive authority levels are defined and a delineated escalation process provides for any exceptions. This design enables competent operators to emerge at this ML. While the jobs may be heavily circumscribed, efficiency results from the accrued competency arising from the repetition of work tasks.

Management is intensely rule-bound. The style starts as directive in the early stages of this ML. It phases to pacesetting as adherence to procedures improves and as competency increases. Instructions thus become less and less necessary. The blueprint that may have been apparent (to the outside observer) at ML1a has all but faded by now (see Baron and Burton, 1999 and 2002). As the organisation grows in size and ages, and as external stakeholders exert influence on the design and style of the firm, the bureaucratic form of enterprise predominates.

Decision-making is goal-oriented for managers. The goals will be focused on establishing and maintaining efficiency and control. Employees, in general, are not required to make decisions at this ML. They are expected to know their jobs and do their jobs as prescribed.

The organisational climate is dominated by process discipline. There is a strong atmosphere of bureaucracy that instills risk aversion.

OML2b – Process Management: Organisation-Wide

The organisation can now build on the experience and learning that arose at ML2a. Managers learn the road to efficiency at ML2a and come to realise that there are further gains available through standardisation across the *whole* organisation. Continuing with diverse local practices means that the organisation as a whole misses out on such opportunities. In all other respects, this ML is the same as ML2a.

So, the 'one best way' in each process area and for each work practice from across all the units is adopted by all units. For instance, the best project management methodology is adopted, the best logistics dispatch practice is implemented and the best pricing tools are used etc.

As an aside, it should be noted that without the experience of crafting their own work practices at ML2a, managers and employees would not learn of the value of taking a systematic approach to work organisation. Through the experience at ML2a, managers come to appreciate the advantages of efficiency. They realise that further gains are available through pooling intelligence across the whole organisation. The business cannot simply leap from ML1 to ML2b. Imposing a 'one best way' on all units would fail without first gaining the learning at ML2a.

As a consequence of taking a common approach to common work practices, a unified climate or culture starts to emerge at ML2b (Curtis et al, p.24).

OML3 – Proficiency Management

The focus of the firm now shifts to continuous improvement (CI). This is a move from efficiency to proficiency for systems, processes and people. To relieve the pressure on the CEO, as we will describe below, a new tier is created – the strategic business unit (SBU). Not surprisingly, the measures of effectiveness at OML3 are beating the competition, increasing market share and above-benchmark financial results.

At this ML, explicit strategies arise. There are three levels of strategy at ML3: for the enterprise as a whole, for each SBU and for each function in each SBU. All cover the medium term. Plans are informed by external benchmarking and external experts may be sought out to help devise such plans. However, these strategies are loosely coupled: between the functional and that for the SBU; between the SBU and the enterprise strategy; across SBUs; across different functions in any one SBU; and between the same functions across all the SBUs. This loose coupling renders all of these pseudo-strategies largely operational in nature. Above all else, the overall enterprise strategy is best described as embryonic at this maturity level.

As a system, the company is partially open. The external benchmarking and the search for best practice open up managers and employees to outside ideas.

Work practices are lean. Processes are systematically measured and re-engineered to drive CI. Tools such as Lean and Six Sigma belong here. They may appear at lower maturity levels, but they are not truly exploited until ML3 (Curtis et al, p.25). Thus, a whole host of management tools are imported or homegrown to support CI.

The creation of strategies means that project management now evolves into 'programme management'. Medium-term programmes consisting of a range of individual but aligned projects are designed. These are systematically tracked to ensure delivery on time, to cost and to specification. To manage this tracking, a Programme Management Office (PMO) is established. Programmes tend to consist of big change projects at this ML. In terms of operational arrangements and programme management, each SBU and major function indulges in forecasting its own activities. Such forecasting is an early attempt by the organisation to gain some control over its environment. This is, as yet, only loosely coordinated across the functions and SBUs.

The organising principle takes on a new dimension at ML3. SBUs, with their own General Managers, are organised by market. Market may be defined by product or by geography. Within each SBU, however, the organising principle remains functional. Thus, the structure of the overall enterprise resembles the multidivisional structure, the so-called M-form, while the structure of each division will resemble the uniform structure or so-called U-form. Where authority is substantially delegated to SBUs leaving the enterprise to focus purely on financial targets, the enterprise structure may even resemble that of a holding company or H-form.

Each SBU General Manager and her heads of function have greater autonomy than at ML2 – they effectively define their own (divisional and functional) strategies. However, unlike at ML2, the structure at ML3 is flat or delayered in nature. Vertical accountability levels are defined. Even in the largest of organisations, there are only a maximum of seven accountability levels. Examples of these are described in Table 4.

The delayering allows staff previously 'in the line' at ML2 to be redeployed to programmes and projects. This delayering provides the 'slack' necessary to resource the focus on continuous improvement.

The divisional/functional structure still requires coordination. Relying upon the enterprise-level CEO to deliver this alone would fail (this reliance on the CEO is a key constraint at ML2). Common financial deliverables relieve her of much of the day-to-day coordination. Each SBU is charged with delivering common, standard financial targets. This allows the CEO to assess the overall performance of each division. Within each divisional SBU, each GM coordinates using Service Level Agreements (SLA). Internal and external customer expectations are gathered to ensure SLAs deliver to meet these expectations. The CEO's residual management task is to manage the inherent contradictions and conflicts between the SBU, functional and enterprise strategies and programmes.

Jobs are now designed so that they are moderately broad. In essence, vertical specialisation is reduced through the decentralisation of authority and the delayered structure. There is much better role-functional-divisional alignment. However, as described above, alignment between the enterprise

Table 4. Accountability Levels			
Level	*Example Role*	*Accountability*	*Time Horizon*
VII	Global CEO	To deliver value through developing the configuration of the global portfolio of businesses and assets	10–15 years
VI	President, EMEA	To deliver the annual and strategic plans through integrating a network or group of separate (level V) companies and developing the 'opportunity space'*, e.g. market entry or exit	5–10 years
V	Vice President, UK	To deliver the annual and strategic plans for a standalone business, in the specific 'opportunity space'* through optimising the allocation of resources and through targeted innovations	5 years
IV	Manufacturing Director, UK	To establish, maintain and develop the infrastructures in order to deliver the annual and strategic plans	3–5 years
III	Factory Manager	To develop the capability of current processes and infrastructures through integrating different functional activities	Up to 18 months
II	First Line Manager	To ensure the task delivery through a team of level I workers and through flexing the work schedules	Schedule horizon of no more than 3 months
I	Production Worker	To deliver products or services to the prescribed specification	Task cycle of no more than 3 months

* 'opportunity space' is the territory, technology or product that an operating business unit is assigned, e.g. a national market for car production and sales. It specifies the boundaries that defines WBAWI and also 'what business are we not in'.

and the divisional SBUs is narrow – based upon a limited range of financial targets. Building upon the competent operators that we saw at ML2a, competent teams are emergent at this stage of development.

The pacesetting management style is, at first, inherited from ML2b. As ML3 becomes increasingly consolidated, the style phases to (performance) coaching. As individual competency improves, and as CI is embedded in the organisation, managers move towards supporting functional CI through the coaching of their subordinates.

CI demands meticulous measurement. What is most noticeable about a firm at this maturity level is the abundance of Key Performance Indicators (KPI). Input, process and output metrics are everywhere. The profusion of KPIs supports short-interval performance management. This is facilitated by best-in-class management information systems (MIS) for each function. Each MIS is designed to provide management information for control and decision-making (MICAD). Hence, decision-making is data-driven. The profusion of data and associated analysis means that managers are guided by these metrics.

The organisational climate exudes the pursuit of functional excellence. Risk-taking is now encouraged as it is informed by good data and clear accountability.

OML4 – Systematic Management

The focus of the company now moves to 'viability' in the specific sense used in the viable systems model (VSM). Viability is defined as the ability to maintain a separate existence and maintain internal stability despite living in an unpredictable external environment. As we describe this maturity level, it will be clear that all previous levels do not ensure viability for various reasons.

Building upon the firm's experience at ML3, it is able to identify the core activities and core competences (including synergies) that best support its own viability. Non-core activities are outsourced, so retaining only the strategically valuable skills in-house. Organisations thus concentrate on what they are good at – where they can excel over rivals.

Thus, the measures of effectiveness at OML4 are cultural cohesion, high employee morale, low turnover, personal development and teamwork.

There is, at this ML, a long-term, integrated enterprise strategy. This is informed by comprehensive environmental scanning that searches for any potential discontinuities, which may imply the need for internal adjustments to deal with such shocks. The vision and values of the organisation are explicit and also validated. This validation links back to a clear understanding of the firm's core competences and value-added chain. The culture becomes part of the management system as a form of normative control.

As a system, and as a viable system, the organisation is open. The external scanning of the company's various environments (internal, as well as external) and the existence of an integrated enterprise strategy are necessary conditions for viability.

The enterprise goes beyond work practices. It now seeks to establish and maintain world-class, end-to-end business processes regardless of functional considerations. Process owners, thus, come to the fore.

Project management takes a further evolutionary leap at this level. The explicit enterprise strategy is supported by portfolio management, with programmes and projects embedded hierarchically within the portfolio. The PMO evolves into the Office for Strategic Management (OSM) as the guardian of the portfolio and the supporting methodologies. In general, however, change is incremental with techniques such as Kaizen enabling frequent improvements. Process re-engineering and project management are 'in the line'. The 'slack' that was reserved as an offline resource at ML3 is now built back into the line in self-managed teams (SMT).

The combination of an integrated strategy, environmental scanning and the OSM enables the whole organisation to practise a more sophisticated level of end-to-end forecasting. This minimises the danger of external shock disrupting the internal arrangements of the firm.

The organisation structure takes on a flexible principle. This has been called the 'lattice' structure. In a sense, this is a misnomer as it is not a structure in a traditional sense. In reality, no single organisational structure predominates overall and the organisation flexes, temporarily, to meet the demands of the time. Project teams arise, are generally self-directed and fade away as the temporary need is fulfilled. Virtual teams fit comfortably at this ML. Coordination is through liaison devices. These liaison devices are designed to manage the 'white space' between the blocks on the organisation chart. We will study the 'lattice structure' and liaison devices in more detail in chapter four.

Coordination is also pushed to the lowest level possible in the organisation. The design is 'bottom up' from a host of SMT. These may be permanent, as on the production line, or they may be temporary, as with a project team. Operators are multi-skilled to support the SMT concept. They are empowered to make decisions appropriate for their accountabilities. Subject matter experts (SME) are available to support the SMT as and when necessary.

Job design now aims to build roles, not jobs. Roles are dynamic and grow with the competency of the occupant. There is now clear role-organisational alignment, from unified vision through competencies to each individual role.

The management style becomes fully participative, encouraging collaboration. This is in line with the SMT concept mentioned earlier. There are elements of the visionary style, especially from senior management, as the strategy is now explicit and enterprise-wide and all roles play a part in delivering that strategy.

Decision-making is systemic. That is, it takes the whole of the enterprise into consideration, building upon the process-perspective characteristic of this maturity level. All decisions are guided by and further the vision and values.

The organisational climate would be recognised as a high-performance culture – an agile organisation. An air of 'responsible autonomy' pervades the firm.

A summary of the organisational maturity levels is set out in Table 5.

Properties of Maturity Models

There are some properties of all maturity models, and the HRMM in particular, that should be noted at this stage in the discussion.

An organisation can only operate at one maturity level in any sustainable manner. The implementation of work practices will not be feasible if they belong to several maturity levels. Practices at any one ML are self-supporting and self-reinforcing. They are, in essence, compatible and complementary. If a business endeavours to launch a practice that, say, belongs to a much higher ML, the internal environment will not be conducive to sustainable success. Further, attempting to operate at more than one ML will place unendurable pressure upon the organisation and its employees. This 'mix-and-match' approach to selecting work practices is thus a doomed project.

Improvement plans that progress to the next higher ML are, however, possible. This is feasible if all the practices in the lower ML have been fully *institutionalised* (Curtis et al, p.52). Essentially, each ML acts as the foundation for the next higher level. All the foundations need to be firmly in place before progression to the next higher level can be successfully attempted. Otherwise, implementation is in great danger of failure.

Table 5. Organisational Maturity Levels – Summary

	ML1a	ML1b	ML2	ML3	ML4
Focus	Launch & survive Make & sell	Consolidate market position and growth	Efficiency Stability Internal control	Continuous improvement	Viability
Measures of effectiveness	NPD rates Creative solutions Growth	NPD rates Creative solutions Growth	Efficiency Timeliness Consistency Reliability	Beating the competition Market share growth Financial results	Cultural cohesion Employee morale Low turnover Personal development Teamwork
Strategy	Exploratory Implicit	Implicit Phantom document	Implicit Operational Short-term	Divisional SBU and functional Embryonic loosely coupled enterprise strategy External benchmarking Medium-term	Integrated enterprise strategy Environmental scanning Vision and values in use Long-term
System	Very open Exposed	Moderately open	Closed	Partially open	Open
Work practices	Trial and error approach No standardisation	Erratic Variable, volatile performance Statutory compliance Accountancy controls	SOPs SOFP Change control process	Lean Basic forecasting	World-class business processes Advanced forecasting
Project management	None	Ad hoc	Basic methodology	Programme management PMO	Portfolio management OSM

Structure	Fluid Direct control by founder	Archaic or evolving No 'organising principle' Coordination by founder/managers	U-form Functional 'organising principle' Competent management teams Operational coordination by CEO	M-form Divisional SBUs Functional within the SBU Flat/delayered Accountability levels Coordination by SLA within divisions Operational coordination by GMs Enterprise coordination by CEO	Flexible 'lattice' structure Coordination by strategy, liaison devices and SMT
Job design	None 'Muck in' 'Muddle through'	Ambiguous jobs	Narrow Limited authority levels below CEO Defined escalation process Competent operators	Moderately broad jobs Emergent competent teams	Broadening roles SMT
Management style	Personality of founder	Heroic Inconsistent	Rule-bound Directive phasing to pacesetting	Pacesetting phasing to coaching	Participative Visionary
Decision-making style	Gut-feel	Gut-feel	Goal-oriented	Data-driven	Systemic
Climate	Personality of founder	Compliance Irresponsible autonomy	Process discipline Bureaucratic	Functional excellence	High performance culture Agile organisation Responsible autonomy

There are a series of institutionalisation practices that ensure any one work practice is firmly in place in the business. These are set out in Table 6 (Curtis et al, p.60-63).

Energy and resources are required to advance from one ML to the next. This can be likened to a phase transition in physics, i.e. the energy or latent heat required to phase from liquid to gas. There will be a dynamic tension in the organisation as it phases from one ML to the next.

It follows from what has been said so far that, in general, there is no option to skip an ML and, in particular, to advance to ML4 in one go. This represents the 'world-class-in-one-leap' fallacy. If the foundations of all the lower levels are not in place, this approach is doomed to failure. Improvement plans are thus best crafted as consisting of 'single gap actions' (Verweire et al, p.290-291) – that is, plans should focus on the consolidation of practices at the current ML and then on the progression to the next higher ML. There are forces that restrain the organisation at the current level and forces that encourage advancement. These forces are in dynamic tension and hold the firm in a quasi-equilibrium.

Each level is self-reinforcing, as we have said. All the practices at a given ML are complementary. The pattern of practices tends to define the climate as we have seen earlier in this chapter. Hence, there is a built-in resistance *against* advancing to the next higher ML. This is reinforced by the very fact that the measure of effectiveness at any one ML is implicitly defined as the full implementation and institutionalisation of the work practices at *that* level. For example, when efficiency is established at ML2b, it will be hard for internal agents to see how this could be improved upon, given the implicit focus of the organisation at that level.

Thus, for the business to move on, it has to break free, as it were, from its current organisational climate. The firm has to reinvent itself, again and again, to progress to ML4. This is feasible as there are countervailing forces built into each maturity level.

Thus, conversely, there are internal and external pressures at each level that spur the enterprise to the next level. As other commentators have identified, there are crises built into each stage of development that must be addressed in order for the business to progress. The next higher level is, in essence, a solution to the crises at the preceding level. For example, the apparent chaos that ensues at ML1b is solved by the strict centralised control imposed by the one general manager, the CEO, and the SOPs at ML2. The crisis of operational coordination at ML2 is resolved by the granting of autonomy to divisions built

Table 6. Institutionalisation Practices	
Policy statement	The organisational commitment to guiding principles and/or behaviours in a given work practice area
Coordinating role	Role(s) with the assigned responsibility to coordinate activities at the organisational level Defines common procedures or assists units to define their own Reviews unit activities to ensure compliance Collects and shares experience across all units Provides advice as required The style of approach will differ according to the maturity level, e.g. advisory at ML2a
Funding and resources	Provision of funds, resources, materials, equipment, specialised skills and time to perform the activities
Skills to perform work practices	Provision of learning interventions to give the employees required to carry out the work practices the necessary specialised skills
Orientation to understand work practices	The provision of information to employees who need to know about the work practice These employees may be affected by the specific work practice in some way and thus require an understanding of the work practice
Documentation	Work practices are clearly defined and documented, covering some or all of the following: Policy statement (see above) Procedural steps Guidelines for managers Authority levels, roles and responsibilities Forms to progress procedures and authorise action
Plans to maintain work practice	The managerial commitment to create and follow a plan to implement and maintain the relevant work practices
Measurement	Metrics and other measurements to indicate: The extent of implementation of the work practices across the unit/organisation The effectiveness and/or efficiency of the work practices in any one unit to identify the need for corrective action and improvement
Verification of compliance to policy	The process assurance that work practices comply with policy and regulations, conducted by a person assigned that responsibility
Executive reviews	To provide insight to work practices at senior levels To provide overall governance of the policy and associated work practices

into ML3. The second crisis of strategic coordination at ML3 is dissipated by the integrated enterprise strategy and normative controls that are developed at ML4. Thus, there are cycles of 'control–chaos–control' throughout the maturity model as a whole. The nature of those controls, however, differs enormously. In fact, the implicit definition of 'control' is different at each ML.

External constraints and forces may either stimulate progression or hold it back. So, a dominant external coalition may force the organisation rigidly to abide by regulations. This may trap the firm in a bureaucratic web, characteristic of ML2b. On the other hand, the acquisition of a smaller enterprise operating at ML1b may stimulate the move to ML2 in order to match the demands of the new parent company.

Given that energy and resource are needed to move eventually to ML4, some may prefer, consciously or sub-consciously, to settle for a lower level. This is highly likely to arise, given the inertia that holds an organisation at its current ML. However, it should be clear that the only level that is viable in the long run is ML4. Ironically, this is the only stable level because it is an agile state. All other levels are not stable states in terms of viability. They are all vulnerable to external and (sometimes) internal shock. Without continual and ecological renewal, a firm is in danger of becoming stale, outdated and, ultimately, moribund.

However, progress is by no means guaranteed. As we have seen, stagnation at the current ML is likely, but slippage back to a lower ML is also a possibility. All systems decay into inertia and entropy where attention and investment are lacking. Energy is required to maintain a maturity level. Regression is also possible if the firm is subject to an external shock. A sudden loss of cash or the failure of a new product could make work practices of higher maturity levels no longer affordable and sustainable. The firm may then, in effect, retrench at a lower ML. Such retrenchment tends to be messy as practices of a higher ML are dismantled and replaced. The sense of urgency around such reforms exacerbates the issues.

Finally, we must make it clear that the concept of maturity is not a surrogate for organisational size or age. While younger, smaller enterprises may tend to reflect the characteristics of lower maturity levels, this is coincidental. Conversely, larger, older firms, even multinational firms have been known to be locked into ML1b. Smaller, younger firms have the ability and speed to attain ML4. For all enterprises, it is a matter of continuous improvement, conscious choice and investment.

HR Maturity Levels

We may now turn to the specific work domain of HR – the subject of the book. For every organisational maturity level (OML), there is a commensurate HR maturity level (HRML) that supports and complements that OML. The high-level picture is set out in Table 7.

Table 7. Organisational and HR Maturity Levels		
	Organisational Maturity Level	*HR Maturity Level*
ML1	Entrepreneurial Management	Initial
ML2	Process Management	Foundational
ML3	Proficiency Management	HR Agenda
ML4	Systematic Management	Integrated People Strategy

In this section, we will give a brief overview of each HRML. The details will be explored in depth in individual chapters later. The general characteristics we will deal with here are set out in Table 8. These characteristics form, what in the literature is often called, the HR operating model. We will explore this operating model in chapter 12 in more detail.

Table 8. Human Resource Maturity Levels – Characteristics
Nature of HR strategy
Drivers of HR activity
Time horizons
Prime HR practice(s)
Predominant HR organisational role

HRML1 – Initial Level

To match the OML, there are two phases at ML1. At HRML1a, specialist HR personnel are absent. The firm is so new and small that it does not warrant specialist staffing. This may apply to other professional support staff as well, e.g. marketing. HR activities are spread across various employees in an ad hoc manner. The founder herself may do much of the work that later may be assigned to HR. External support may be sought where the technical demands of the situation necessitate such specialist input. The only foundational HR processes at HRML1a are payroll-related; that is, from hours worked to gross pay and from gross pay to net pay (see Table 9).

As the company grows in size, the need for internal specialist support becomes recognised. Again, this will not be unique to HR. The focus of the newly hired HR staff is on compliance, primarily to external requirements, e.g. employment law. Where a trade union or works council is in place, compliance will also be to relevant agreements.

The focus of HR at HRML1b is on being legal, honest and decent. Managers will consider HR work to be administrivia and so palm it off onto the HR staff (Curtis et al, p.19). There is no HR strategy and few standard procedures. There will be a feeling of reinventing the wheel every time a familiar HR task arises.

HR's work is event-driven, if not incident-driven. In common with the rest of the organisation, HR appears to be dealing with a series of random crises. The time horizon is thus very short-term.

There is no prime HR practice at ML1. HR has to deal with anything and everything as it arises, when it arises.

HR's predominant roles are that of compliance police and firefighter.

HRML2 – Foundational Level

In common with the rest of the company, there is no explicit HR strategy at ML2 (rewards is a slight exception to this rule – see below). The focus of HR at this level is to establish repeatable HR practices. Efficiency is achieved throughout the organisation through this administrative approach, and HR is no exception to this rule. As with the wider business, this is done at the unit level at ML2a, while at ML2b, this is done across the entire organisation.

As mentioned, the exception is reward practices. Where these differ widely across a single business, a sense of inequity arises. This is characteristic of ML1. To avoid this, at ML2a, reward practices are standardised across the whole business (Curtis et al, 2002, p.32). Thus, compensation and benefit (C&B) policies *and* practices are common at ML2a. However, this will not amount to a true C&B strategy as such, as it is not based upon any guiding principles or employer brand.

HR's version of SOPs will be the policies and procedures covering the foundational HR processes, at least. These processes are summarised in Table 9. We will revisit each of these in more detail in later chapters. These foundational processes capture the 'rights and rules' and the procedures to enact them. This builds on the compliance role we first encountered at ML1b. Employees have rights. These derive from entitlements in the contract of employment, convention, statutory rights and those derived from company procedures *and* the implied right to organisational justice. In addition, HR collates the internal and external rules. All of these are captured in some policy and procedure manual, hard copy and/or online.

HR is internally focused on establishing and maintaining HR efficiency. This requires the codification, standardisation, enforcement and reinforcement of HR policies and procedures. The work is thus highly routine, transactional in nature and heavily bureaucratic. This aligns with the climate of the wider organisation at ML2. Consequently, this introspection means that the link between HR policies and added-value for the organisation is, at best, tenuous and generally obscure at this maturity level.

HR is procedurally driven and the perspective is short-term. As cases arise, HR identifies the relevant procedure, the rights and entitlements invoked by the case and advises the manager and/or employee accordingly. Exceptions are escalated and used to amend current policies or invent new ones as appropriate.

We will see in chapter five that the prime HR practice at ML2 is recruitment. The greatest effect on enhancing the overall performance of the business is through new hires (Curtis et al, 2002, p.31).

HR's prime role is that of a service provider. These services centre on the foundational HR processes (see Table 9); in particular, recruitment and basic change management. In addition, HR take on the role of employee advocacy. This arises as employee rights are enshrined in the HR policies and procedures. HR often has to educate line managers so that these rights are not infringed.

HRML3 – HR Agenda

Similar to the wider enterprise, HR now has an explicit functional HR strategy. The perspective shifts to the medium term. HR seeks best-in-class solutions to the HR problems of the business. However, the implementation of this HR strategy is adapted to align with the array of SBU and functional strategies characteristic of ML3. Each SBU GM has to be accommodated, so HR practices still differ across SBUs.

As with the host organisation, HR is also focused on continuous improvement (CI). KPIs abound and these metrics are used to guide CI

Table 9. Foundational HR Processes		
HR Pillar	*HR Process*	*Comments*
Organisational Effectiveness	Job Description design	
	Organisational charts	Defining reporting lines and team structures
	Core management responsibilities	
	Communications pack template	To manage each specific proposed critical change event
Calibre and talent	Resourcing and selection	Personnel Requisition Form (PRF) to authorise the hiring process Person specification Internal and external appointment procedures
	Starter procedure	
	Rostering	To 'manage time' by defining working time, assigning shifts, setting start times, breaks etc.
	Attendance policy and procedure	To manage planned and unplanned absences, rehabilitation plans and returns to work
	Leavers procedures	All types of exit, e.g. disciplinary, capability, redundancy, retirement etc.
Employee engagement	Communications	Basic communication tools, e.g. noticeboards, basic meeting techniques
	Grievance procedure	
Performance management systems	Budgets and objectives procedures	The processes of setting annual targets
	'Works' rules	To regulate behaviour through defining general responsibilities, duties and prohibitions for all employees
	Disciplinary procedure	
	Performance improvement plan (PIP) guidelines	
Employee development	Basic job training	To establish operational effectiveness
	First line manager training	Covering core management responsibilities

Reward and recognition	Grading	Job sizing processes
	Terms & conditions matrix	
	Salary and contract change process	Payroll control form to authorise changes to basic pay and contractual terms
	Contract of employment	
	Initial offer pack	
	Annual pay review process	
	Payroll (1)	From hours worked to gross pay
	Payroll (2)	From gross pay to net pay

projects and make the function proficient. A supportive HRIS provides data for MICAD. The internal customer is a key player, but at this ML, this is mainly the line manager.

As a service function, the key metrics are: reliability, empathy, relevance and responsiveness. *Reliability* is a measure of the ability to perform the service with diligence and accuracy. *Empathy* is a measure of the caring individualised treatment of the actual client of the service. *Relevance* is a measure of how useful the client finds the service in meeting her needs. *Responsiveness* is a measure of the promptness and timeliness of the delivery to meet the client's needs.

The prime HR practice at this maturity level centres around the performance management system. The CI agenda and the proliferation of KPIs demands sophisticated tools to drive improvement forward.

At this ML, the primary role of HR is that of advisor – as an expert in organisation, people and people management.

HRML4 – Integrated People Strategy

There is now an integrated enterprise strategy. The perspective is on the long-term with the vision and values guiding HR in strategic planning. There is less of a people strategy and more people themes and content running throughout the overall enterprise strategy.

HR is intelligence-led. The data built up at ML3 enables HR to contribute to the identification and embedding of the core competences. From this the strategy map for the whole organisation has been built to inform all aspects of its people practices. Best practice is benchmarked externally and internal customers, managers *and* employees now inform people policies.

The capability of line management now allows HR, or rather people management practices, to operate 'in the line'. This was not possible at lower maturity levels.

The prime HR practice is the vision and values. These guide all other HR practices, but especially competency development for each employee. Employee development thus has a high profile in HR terms at this ML.

HR's role now moves to that of a strategic (people) partner. This role is values-driven. The values inform competencies and the procedure-driven character of ML2 is now fully replaced by the principles-driven nature of the function. HR takes on the mantle of organisational conscience and cultural guardian, thus reinforcing the organisational climate at this ML.

Summary

In this chapter, we explained the nature of maturity models before exploring the general nature of the HRMM. We described a maturity model as a systematic methodology for raising the capability of work practices in a specific domain. In our case, we are interested in HR (work) practices. We then defined the four generic maturity levels of any and every firm – the organisational maturity levels (OML), from start-up to systematic management. We saw how the purpose of the business is implicit at all maturity levels *below* ML4. We then described the properties of maturity models and how this enables some actions and restricts others on the part of agents in any given organisation. We also outlined the critical role of institutionalisation practices. These are designed to 'lock in' and embed work practices. Finally, we briefly set out each of the four human resource maturity levels (HRML) that complement the four OML.

CHAPTER 3

HUMAN RESOURCE STRATEGIC FRAMEWORK

Introduction

In this chapter, we explore the second axis of the $HRMM_x$. This is the HR strategic framework that consists of six pillars covering the sub-specialisms of HR. We will offer definitions of each of the six pillars. The degree to which any one organisation fulfils these definitions will depend upon the maturity level of that business and of its HR practices. The detailed HR work practices under each pillar will be described in subsequent chapters. Finally, having explored the nature of OML and HRML in the previous chapter, we will be able to draw the $HRMM_x$, which combines the maturity levels and the HR pillars.

HR Core Purpose

In general, without a purpose, action is unfocused, random, traditional and probably incoherent. Specifically, without a clear purpose, it is impossible for staff in the HR function to test what activities they should get involved in and what activities are peripheral or irrelevant to their professional practice. Thus, it is impossible to determine how HR can contribute to an organisation's well-being without a clear sense of purpose.

There have been many attempts to define HR, but the statement of core purpose that we have found most useful *and* operational is as follows:

- Raising people and organisational capability and performance

- Enhancing employee satisfaction, significance and balance

- To facilitate the short-, medium- and long-term success of the organisation

The use of the present participle, in this case 'raising', is quite deliberate. There is no endgame strategically, only a direction. Strategic development is an ongoing journey. Plans may have finite timescales, but the strategic purpose is unending.

HR is not just the people profession, but also the organisational profession. HR 'manages through organisation', not simply through people. The EU defines medium-size enterprises as 51-249 employees. On average, beyond the limit of approximately 150 people, psychologically it becomes increasingly difficult to hold all of the possible social relationships in one's head. Hence, as groups get larger, the personal is replaced by the systematic. However, it should not be forgotten that organisations are populated by people.

The core purpose also focuses on the short through to the long term. Immediate performance is of interest. However, raising current capability proffers the potential for future enhanced performance. Raising current capability is an investment in the future.

The core purpose also reflects the two sides of HR – the constant balance of, and tension between, enterprise and employee needs. Here, we have captured the higher needs of employees in terms of satisfaction, significance and balance. Satisfaction is self-explanatory. Significance is the degree to which the employee feels how well her job, work, performance etc. contribute to the overall purpose of the organisation, the community and, ultimately, the planet. Balance is how much the employee feels that her employment role and all her external roles complement each other, or whether they are in conflict.

Finally, HR has a higher purpose, which is to help the organisation prosper over time. Without success, there is no employment. Without employment, there is no HR!

The HR Strategic Framework

Professionals cannot 'do' HR; they can only 'do' HR practices. Most practices fit into one or other of the generally recognised specialisms of the broader HR profession. Here, we offer a framework consisting of six sub-specialisms. To some extent, any framework is arbitrary. The key question is whether it is useful in practice. The following framework of six pillars has proven to be of practical value in a number of organisations:

- Organisational effectiveness (OE)
- Calibre and talent (C&T)
- Employee engagement (EE)
- Performance management systems (PMS)
- Employee development (ED)
- Rewards and recognition (R&R).

Each of these has its own specific definition, but each sits at one logical level down from the overall core purpose of HR. They do not, however, sit in isolation of each other. Each informs the others and is in turn informed by the other pillars of the HR framework. Below, we set out the definition of each pillar. The detailed HR work practices within each are described in later chapters.

Organisational Effectiveness

"Every organised human activity… gives rise to two fundamental and opposing requirements: the *division of labour* into various tasks to be performed and the *coordination* of those tasks to accomplish the activity. The structure of an organisation can be defined simply as the total of the ways in which its labour is divided into distinct tasks and then its coordination achieved among those tasks." (Mintzberg, 1989, p.100-101).

OE is defined as:

- Configuring role assignments and labour coordination and
- Managing the processes of change
- Building and maintaining role clarity, context and purpose

This will be recognised as the organisational design and development (OD) aspect of HR. It includes the division of labour, the coordination of that labour and structural hierarchy, overall, that is 'managing through organisation'. Organisational structure is, in itself, a vehicle for the deployment of strategy.

Formally, we can dissect the variables of the system that is 'structure'. The larger the size of the market, the greater the scope for division of labour and hence the greater degree of specialisation; the greater the degree of specialisation, the greater the demand for coordination; the higher the need for close supervision, the narrower the span of control for managers. Thus, the higher the need for coordination, the greater the scale of the enterprise and the narrower the average span of control, the greater the requirement for hierarchy, hence 'structure'.

The variable in this 'structure system' that may be least familiar is closeness of supervision. This is affected by the following factors (see Perrow):

- The degree to which tasks are non-routine
- The amount of difference between the expertise of the manager and that of her subordinates
- The amount of interdependence among tasks under one manager
- The interdependence of these tasks with those performed under different managers
- The interdependence of the department as a whole with other departments in the organisation
- The varying kinds of routine and non-routine mixes of the departments
- The degree to which written rules and regulations or machines can reduce the need for personal supervision
- The extent to which flexibility and rapid response is necessary for the organisation.

In a static world, initial design would suffice. However, in reality, change is a constant. OE implies the need for regular reviews and change in order to maintain and enhance effectiveness. No organisational structure is perfect. Structure is, in effect, a two-dimensional solution to a multidimensional problem. So, structures in themselves do not 'solve' all of the problems of the organisation. The division of labour, its coordination and hierarchy cause problems in their own right. Structures thus do not last forever, so change must be managed. How change is managed is a strong signal of the culture of the enterprise. It demonstrates what the organisation 'thinks' of its people. As change pervades all aspects of the firm in general and HR in particular, OE cuts across all the other pillars of the HR framework. It is not just a specialism in itself, it is a core competency for the HR function as a whole.

The nature of job and organisational design determines, to a great extent, the degree to which the employee gains role clarity, his sense of place in the organisation and his purpose. These three factors help the employee gain a degree of meaningfulness. We will see the extent of such meaningfulness at the different levels of maturity later in chapter four.

Calibre and Talent

C&T is described as:

- Defining, attracting, acquiring, deploying, progressing and releasing the workforce and
- Creating a critical mass of performance drivers and change agents
- Offering career opportunities and progression

By definition, organisations only exist if they are populated by people – people of the right calibre. Sourcing and recruiting them is a traditional competency of HR. This is employee resourcing.

The requirement for employees may be an explicit plan – workforce planning (WFP). The degree to which this is a deliberate exercise will depend upon the maturity level of the firm. We will explore this further in chapter five.

Within the total population of employees, there is 'talent'. Talent has been described as 'the difference that makes the difference'. It is the talent that will help the organisation fulfil its purpose and deliver its strategy. The specific definition of 'talent' may vary from company to company. However, the one used here – i.e. performance drivers and change agents – has proven to be useful across a number of organisations. This is the realm of the HR specialism of talent management (TM).

Performance Management Systems

- Deploying organisational intent,
- Regulating individual behaviour and
- Holding employees accountable
- Creating an environment in which each employee can succeed

This has been the aim of all managers and entrepreneurs down the ages. It encompasses the multitude of systems, processes and practices to encourage employees to do the owners' bidding, willingly. As we have seen above, intent may be implicit or explicit; the less explicit, the greater the challenges for alignment.

It is a fair assumption that employees wish to succeed. The extent to which they are able to do so depends upon the environment in which they operate. The organisation and its agents are the prime architects of that environment.

Employee Engagement

EE is defined as:

- Generating 'share of mind' for business messages,
- Securing employee commitment and
- Handling differences and conflict
- Building employee voice and participation and
- Building employee involvement and inclusion

Communications is set in a context of an increasingly crowded world in terms of media. Any organisation is competing with multiple channels of communications, many of which are much more attractive to employees than business messages. The purpose of internal communications is first to gain attention and then to improve the understanding of, and commitment to, business agendas and plans.

EE further aims to secure the commitment of the employee to the enterprise. As we will see in later chapters, the level of commitment differs across the maturity levels.

As with all social entities, harmony is not assured. There are inevitably differences and conflicts embedded in the business and between its various stakeholders. Traditionally, this was the realm of industrial relations. Whether the firm recognises a trade union or not, employee relations, as it is now called, are still relevant.

The counterpart to business communications is employee voice and participation. This is the extent to which employees are consulted collectively over matters of general significance before a managerial decision is made. This may be through a trade union and/or works council.

Employee involvement is the degree to which each individual worker can influence local decisions that personally impact on him. Employee inclusion is the degree to which the internal population is fully and actively representative of the external population in terms of all socially relevant characteristics.

Employee Development

The scope of ED is:

- Raising people capability in terms of knowledge, skills and process abilities
- Establishing personal competence,
- Developing performance excellence and
- Progressing the employee development journey

Knowledge and skills are self-explanatory. Process abilities cover the individual's capacity to sequence or order work correctly in accordance with the prescribed workflow.

There are two levels of personal capability. There is the personal competence required to do the job effectively. This is the level of performance expected after the employee has 'settled in'. Then, there is the stretch standard of excellence or mastery.

Finally, development interventions support the employee life cycle through the firm. The degree to which ED actually does so under each ML will be described in chapter eight.

Rewards and Recognition

The description of R&R is:

- Building competitiveness in the chosen employment market(s),
- Delivering the employment deal(s) and
- Creating vehicles for 'motivational messages'
- Maintaining a 'good' standard of living and
- Attaining 'due' recognition and 'just' deserts

First and foremost, the firm needs to compete in the labour market in order to secure the human capital it requires and desires. Maintaining a competitive position requires the presentation and fulfillment of a credible 'employment deal'. The employer may participate in more than one labour market and may thus offer different employment deals to the different groups of employees that she hires. An 'employment deal' captures all the 'hard' and 'soft' terms of the relationship between the employer and the employee. It is much broader than just compensation & benefits and consists of the expectations each party has about the relationship (see Flynn, 2014). As we will see, in limited circumstances, this may be expressed as an employer brand or an employee value proposition.

Money is the most obvious aspect of any employment deal. However, this is not the only element in the deal. While reward policies and practices focus on salaries, bonuses and benefits, the explicit and implicit promises in any employment deal can stretch far beyond these more tangible rewards. The employer may undertake to train employees, offer them promotion opportunities, permit a high degree of discretion in the execution of work assignments etc. Both parties to the psychological contract have economic, social, emotional, if not spiritual expectations – explicit and implicit. Further, to a greater or lesser degree, the employer wishes to motivate workers to the degree necessary to fulfil work assignments. Hence, whether consciously done or not, the employer transmits 'motivational messages' through the actions of the employer's agents.

The employee, on the other hand, seeks a good standard of living, and fair and equitable recognition and treatment. Such fair treatment applies to all pillars of the HR strategic framework. The employee seeks an employment deal that reflects his 'worth'.

R&R will be discussed in chapter nine. Motivation is much more than pay and rations, so will be covered in chapter 10.

HR Maturity Matrix

We have now scoped the two axes of the $HRMM_x$. On the one hand, we have set out the organisational and HR maturity levels in chapter two, and on the other we have just described the HR strategic framework. The $HRMM_x$ now appears as in Table 10. All practices across this matrix support and complement each other, thus achieving horizontal fit. Vertically, all practices, to a greater or lesser extent, depending upon maturity level, fulfil the definition of the respective strategic pillar, thus achieving internal vertical fit. All practices at lower ML act as foundations for those above. The detailed HR practices will be described in the following chapters. For completeness, as explained in chapter two, external fit is attained by aligning the HRML with the corresponding OML of the client organisation.

Table 10. HR Maturity Matrix							
OML	HRML	OE	C&T	PMS	EE	ED	R&R
Entrepreneurial Management	Initial						
Process Management	Foundational						
Proficiency Management	HR Agenda						
Systematic Management	Integrated People Strategy						

Summary

In this chapter, we defined the core purpose of HR and presented the two sides of HR – that of the employer and that of the employee. We saw that these two sides are in dynamic tension. We then introduced the HR strategic framework and offered definitions of each of the six pillars, from organisational effectiveness through to reward & recognition. The detailed practices under each pillar are set out in later chapters. This then delineates the second axis which allowed us to sketch the $HRMM_x$. In the next six chapters, we populate each cell of the $HRMM_x$ with the specific HR work practices, pillar-by-pillar, that are relevant to each of the four maturity levels.

CHAPTER 4

ORGANISATIONAL EFFECTIVENESS

Introduction

The reader may recall that we defined OE as:

- Configuring role assignments and labour coordination and
- Managing the processes of change
- Building and maintaining role clarity, context and purpose

In this chapter, we will see how structures, roles and change management evolve as the business steps through each of the four maturity levels. We will describe some of the management and HR tools that feature at each ML. The sophistication of such tools increases as the firm progresses. The reader will also be able to evaluate the extent to which a firm fulfils the definition of OE at each ML.

ML1 – Initial

As we saw in chapter two, direction comes straight from the founder himself at OML1a. He is, in essence, CEO and supervisor all in one. The structure remains fluid and jobs are dynamic as the firm and employees search for solutions to their day-to-day challenges on a trial-and-error basis. The business is in constant flux.

As the organisation moves from start-up into the emerging stage of OML1b, a rudimentary management structure arises. However, HR tends to have few organisation design and development (OD) tools to offer. As compliance is the watchword at HRML1, OD tools do not help in this regard. The structure does not follow any organising principle. It may be archaic, inherited from an acquisition or it may reflect the relatively idiosyncratic nature of managers' roles. As a consequence, coordination is haphazard. This is compounded by the lack of a definition of 'management duties' at

ML1. Each manager carries out her role as she sees fit. There is no common approach.

Jobs are ambiguous in design and are crafted around peoples' personal and unique skill sets rather than any methodology. There is no common format or design process to guide the shaping of jobs. At ML1a, employees will draw meaning via the founder's implicit or explicit mission. At ML1b, the ambiguity will undermine meaningfulness.

Change is managed erratically. At best, employees are advised as change happens or even after change has been decided and implementation is underway. This has been described as the 'mushroom approach'. There is no consistency in procedure or method from one change event to the next. Only where there is a need to comply with external regulations or internal union agreements is there any semblance of prior consultation (see chapter seven on Employee Engagement). Even then, it is of a token nature.

ML2 – Foundational

Direction and overall coordination comes from the one general manager – that is, the CEO. The focus is on operational efficiency. HR will be oriented towards supporting process management. As we have already discussed, the organising principle at this ML is functional. The structure resembles the U-form.

The organisation chart emerges as an OE tool in its own right at this maturity level. The chart portrays the functional reporting lines characteristic of this ML. The organisation chart also acts as a key tool in change management (see below). Coordination at this ML is almost exclusively via the CEO. However, no structure manages all the coordination issues in a business. As mentioned above, any structure is a two-dimensional solution to the multidimensional problem of coordination. So, people issues arise in the 'white space' between the boxes on the organisation chart. These may be labelled as 'people problems', necessitating the involvement of the HR team. Thus, HR is engaged in managing issues at the organisational 'boundaries'. In essence, even where there are no unions present, demarcation disputes still arise and need to be resolved (see EE in chapter seven).

Coordination is further aided by building competent management teams. This is accomplished in two ways: firstly, by running competent meetings; secondly, by defining core management responsibilities.

Meeting processes are addressed to improve management productivity. Tools, such as PACER, are adopted to ensure meetings are efficient: each meeting has a clearly stated *purpose*; the formal *agenda* aims to progress that purpose; formal *conduct* rules are laid down to ensure that the purpose and agenda remain the focus; and each member of the meeting is clear as to their explicit *role* in the meeting. We will see in chapter seven that the competent management team meeting is central to employee engagement at this maturity level.

To support the competent management teams, all managers have their core management responsibilities explicitly laid down. A comprehensive example is set out in Table 11. These cover the essential coordination tasks of any manager of people. However, the degree of discretion is severely limited at ML2, especially at more junior levels of management. However, as the default person specification at ML2 is essentially technical, there is a tendency to refer to HR for guidance on executing these core management tasks.

Job design aids the crafting of the narrow, functional jobs that belong at ML2. Efficiency is secured by a high degree of specialisation at ML2. Specialisation is high, both horizontally and vertically. That is, jobs at the same level have a narrow range of tasks. Further, jobs at different hierarchical levels have tightly defined authority levels and closeness of supervision is high. Job analysis is conducted at all maturity levels from ML2 through to ML4. However, the focus is radically different at these three levels. At ML2, the emphasis is on the functional tasks or duties carried out by the job holder. The weight is on the 'doing' of the job.

Thus, as an output from this job analysis, the job description (JD) arises as a tool in its own right. The primary purpose of the JD is to define the detailed tasks and duties of each job. Each job is described in a coherent manner, with all tasks adding up to a meaningful, if narrow, whole. However, the meaning is very task-oriented. Along with the SOP, the prime purpose of the JD is to give clarity to the occupant of her regular duties. The word 'duty' is notably apt at this level.

The secondary purpose of the JD is to inform recruitment and selection activity (see chapter five on C&T). Thirdly, the JD informs job evaluation (see chapter nine on R&R).

This triple purpose of the JD leads to conflict between the diverse aims. Trying to fit all three aims into one document renders it a cumbersome tool. Thus, most companies craft a more concise version. Where a tool has more

Table 11. Core Management Responsibilities		
Responsibility	*Component*	*Definition*
Securing Resources		To secure the resources for the work unit to achieve work commitments
	Budget Setting and Control	To negotiate and manage the budget for the work unit
	Equipment	To identify and secure the necessary equipment, PPE and materials to enable the work unit to carry out its tasks
Measurement and Reporting	Measurement	To run a measurement system for the work unit to monitor the achievements of assigned work commitments
	Reporting	To keep superior managers informed of the progress of such achievements
Staffing		To staff the work unit to meet the workload demands in order to deliver the desired outcomes effectively in terms of cost, quality, time and productivity To determine the shift patterns and working hours to meet the operating window and satisfy the desired outcomes
	Resourcing	To recruit, select and appoint the 'right' person in accordance with the person specification for each position within the budgeted headcount/establishment for the work unit
	Attendance Management	To ensure maximum attendance among employees in the work unit for the hours required and to manage exceptions to full attendance
Performance Management	Workload Allocation	To allocate work assignments (including shifts and working hours) in an efficient, effective and fair manner among the employees of the work unit to meet the desired outcomes in a way that balances skills, effort, physical and mental demands, time, safety, welfare and equity

Performance Management	Tracking	To measure and monitor individual delivery expectations and maintain performance standards & conduct
	Feedback	To inform each individual of his actual performance relative to work commitments
	Corrective Action	To bring unsatisfactory individual performance back in line with expectations through training, counselling, PIP, informal and formal discipline
Employee Development		To equip each member of the work unit team with the knowledge, skills and process abilities to fulfil the process tasks to the required standard To ensure adequate coverage of skills etc. across the members of the work unit team
	Sourcing Training	To identify and source training and development tools, courses and interventions to equip the team with the necessary knowledge, skills and process abilities To identify gaps in learning intervention offerings and to commission new solutions to meet learning needs
Employee Communications		To engage employees through: imparting information accurately, concisely, succinctly, honestly and openly; and through seeking individual contributions to work issues
	Briefing	To brief the work unit team so that each employee is up to date on issues relevant to the work of the team and to each personally as an employee
	Presentation	To inform and/or convince an audience on a specific topic through a persuasive presentation
	Meeting Management	To plan and run a meeting to achieve its purpose through a systematic agenda and appropriate conduct of the session

Employee Relations		To develop and maintain a positive atmosphere within the work unit team, and between the team and other work units
	Management by Walking About (MBWA)	To regularly 'walk the line' in order to see and be seen, and to keep in touch with what is going on To be available to be approached by employees and to listen to their concerns
	Grievances	To deal with concerns and complaints from employees in a fair, equitable and timely manner
Reward & Recognition	Rewards	To recommend appropriate reward and recognition for individual performance and contribution relative to set or agreed work commitments in accordance with reward policies
	Recognition	To express appreciation to each individual in good time for their efforts towards and achievement of work commitments
	Payroll Rules	To ensure that each employee in the work team receives his entitlement to pay, benefits and expenses in accordance with his contract of employment and the company regulations
Problem-solving		To provide solutions to issues and problems as they arise and to anticipate problems that may arise
Peer Relations		Achieve results through cooperation and collaborating with peers and other employees not within the work unit itself
External Liaison		Achieve results through cooperation and collaborating with external agencies, such as consumers, customers, suppliers, shareholders and regulatory authorities
Change Management		Manage the planned changes of any of the above elements in a fair and equitable manner allowing for effective and proportionate consultation and notice

than one purpose, either one aim predominates or, through compromise, none of the three aims are met. It is therefore not uncommon for the style of JD to rotate around these three conflicting aims over time.

Jobs are standardised as much as possible. Roughly 80 per cent of employees will be covered by 20 per cent of the actual JDs. So, for instance, 'operator', 'driver', 'shop assistant' etc. will have common generic JDs. The actual documentation will also be standard with a common style and format.

Change management is now a basic disciplined process in its own right. At ML2, change is regarded as managing one-off 'critical change events'. Such events are defined as: any event or management action that is (or will be) perceived to threaten the security, status, prosperity or valued working conditions of a group of employees.

To manage such critical change events, management use relevant change tools to plan and execute the change. We call the basic tool a 'communication pack'. This acts as a control document and contains all the communiqués, consultation scripts, letters, timetables and legal requirements to implement the 'specific proposal' (SP). The specific proposal sets out the detailed 'what' and the 'how' of the proposed change. All involved in managing the change then know their particular role in carrying out consultation and communication to implement the SP. The authority level of each manager involved is also set out in the communications pack. The plan takes into account the need for any statutory consultation, e.g. works councils or union negotiations. The communication pack also contains any proposed social plan to assist employees through the transition that may be part of the consultation or negotiations.

ML3 – HR Agenda

As we saw in chapter two, at ML3, organisational direction comes mainly from the SBU and functional strategies and the focus is on continuous improvement. This is reinforced by the fact that, for most employees, the structure remains functional at this ML. We saw that the SBUs are headed by General Managers, tasked with hitting performance targets and driving CI agendas. Coordination is established operationally by the GMs and by service level agreements (SLA) at the boundaries of the functions. Strategically, the CEO endeavours to resolve the contradictions and conflicts that arise from and between the different levels of 'strategies'. The overall shape of the organisation shifts to the M-form.

The creation of SBUs and the appointment of GMs indicate a fair degree of delegation from HQ to the SBUs. However, at ML3, this is an unstable equilibrium. In reality, enterprises at ML3 alternate between decentralisation and centralisation. Initially, HQ grants a degree of autonomy to the SBUs. HQ acts almost as a holding company. However, over time HQ becomes nervous about performance delivery – straying from the narrow financial concerns of a holding company. Further, anxiety rises over the fragmentation of the overall enterprise. Authority is then reined back into the centre. A business may go through several cycles of decentralisation-centralisation-decentralisation etc. There is thus an inherent tension embedded in the design of the M-form.

Functional (or horizontal) clarity was established in the structure at ML2 through the U-form structure and the narrow job design. Hierarchical or vertical clarity is now established at ML3. As we saw in chapter two, accountability levels are defined and a flat structure achieved. A higher level in management is not merely there to supervise the next level below; there is no added value in doing so. Each level in the hierarchy adds value in its own unique way by resolving ever-more complex problems and focusing on a different time horizon. Even in the largest of global businesses, there are only seven unique levels of work, hierarchically speaking (see Table 4). In smaller organisations, there may be less than seven levels with one managerial layer fulfilling the role of, say, three hierarchical levels in Table 4. However, if there are more than seven layers in the organisational hierarchy, responsibilities will be blurred due to overlapping accountabilities. This confusion persists at ML2, but is resolved at ML3.

OD work supports the identification of accountability levels and the consequential changes in roles and structure managed (see below). The precision of role design established at ML2 now moves to a higher level of sophistication. The JD at ML2 listed the inventory of regular tasks an employee had to fulfil. At ML3, jobs evolve into roles. Jobs are static and have clear, rigid boundaries. Roles are dynamic. The SBU and functional strategies and the accountability levels mean that the organisation can identify how each role contributes to the success of the SBU. There is good SBU-function-role alignment. This was absent at ML2. Each role is thus now purposeful in a wider sense than at ML2. The delayering also enables roles to become moderately broad compared to the narrow jobs at ML2. However, the purpose of a role at ML3 is delivery of results.

So, job analysis shifts away from tasks at ML3. The emphasis is on the outputs of a role – that is, the results of job performance. Hence, the JD is now replaced by what we call a role, responsibility, authority and accountability statement (RRAA). As we mentioned in chapter two, the prime HR practices at ML3 derive from the performance management system. The RRAA statement is primarily a PMS tool. An example template for the RRAA is set out in Table 12.

Table 12. Role, Responsibility, Authority and Accountability Statement			
Name:		*Role Title:*	
Area of Responsibility	Activity	Authority	Accountability
What is the title of this area?	What does the occupant of the role do in this area?	What decisions may the occupant make without referral to a higher role?	In this area, what does the organisation hold the occupant accountable for?
Area #1			
Area #2			
Area #3			
Area #4			

To populate the RRAA, the following checklist may be followed:

1. What does the occupant of the role do (activities/tasks)?
2. For each task, what specifically does the business hold the occupant accountable for?
3. For each accountability, as defined, to what extent does the occupant have the authority to deliver that accountability, without referral to or permission from others?
   3.1 If the match between accountability and authority is less than 70 per cent, then redefine the accountability more precisely or
   3.2 Permit greater authority (return to 2 or 3 above)
4. Finally, given all of the above, what is the coherent and consistent purpose of the role as a whole (responsibility)?

The RRAA statement feeds PMS tools (see chapter six). From the above checklist, it should be clear that authority constrains accountability. Accountabilities are frequently overstated. For example, an HR Director may be charged with 'developing and implementing the people strategy'. However, she may not actually have the authority to decide this without referral to, and with the agreement of, the board of directors. So, at ML3, more precision is applied using the RRAA statement. The HR Director's accountability may thus be rewritten as: 'define, agree and deploy the HR strategy through a rolling 3-year plan presented and approved at the company annual planning summit each September'. The word 'agree' explicitly acknowledges the authority of the board of directors. 'Deploy' recognises that the implementation of the strategy will involve managers and employees over whom the HR Director does not have direct authority. The 'plan' gives a clear timescale and explicitly establishes the requirement to deliver a document for board approval with a specific deadline.

Change is now seen as a programme of transition curves, occasionally punctuated by change events (so-called 'punctuated flux'). Each change event initiates a separate transition curve that is, in itself, systematically managed. Each phase of the transition curve is also managed, including the recovery plan (RP). Change is now seen not simply as the implementation of a new structure, for instance, but as a planned transition designed to improve performance. In effect, the purpose of change management is repositioned:

- To manage 'critical change events' and transitions
- so that organisational health, welfare and performance (broadly defined) are enhanced after the transition rather than before
- with minimal trauma experienced through the transition and beyond.

That is, as someone once put it, so the 'gain is worth the pain'.

The phases of the transition are thus managed in detail. An example of this process of facilitated transitions is set out in Table 13.

We call this approach at this ML the 'intermediate change management', so as to distinguish it from the basic approach at ML2. Along with the wider organisation, the perspective shifts to the medium term. Informed by the 'strategies', management consults on plans that are yet to be finalised in detail. Hence, they consult on what we call 'statements of intent' (SOI). This is the confirmation of the intention to change some critical aspect of the business in the future. The proposed endgame is firm and the broad impact upon employees clear, but timescales and details have not yet been pinned down. Thus, management communicates and consults on not just the detailed 'what' and 'how', as with an SP, but the 'big what' of change.

Table 13. Management of the Phases of the Transition Curve	
Phase	*Actions*
Shock	Prior preparation for change Communication pack Consultation and involvement in prior planning Announcement follows a strict structure: introduction; background; rationale; proposals; next steps Communication is formal and ritualistic Consultation but not dialogue (as this draws predictable anger) Allow time away from work area for employees to absorb the message
Denial	Conflict is handled through formal consultation A personal copy of the announcement is issued to potentially-affected staff Update communications on a regular basis, even where there is no new news to give Repeat change messages Keep to the timetable to minimise time of ambiguity but allow time for meaningful consultation Overt denials should be challenged but in a supportive manner Concentrate efforts on delivering the 'day job'
Depression	Consultation agreed or exhausted Support from third party for those exiting Support for cases of extreme depression Acknowledge feelings Take early actions to demonstrate the new reality Informal communications focused on listening Provide space for grieving Provide further information about the new reality Help identify new options and benefits Recovery plan to be agreed in detail by the management team
Acceptance	Remove symbols of the past, respectfully Mark endings with respectful rituals Bring the best of the past forward to the future, but lose the rest Let people take souvenirs and mementoes as appropriate Formal communications focus on the benefits of the new future Performance targets set as achievable Highlight deadlines

Testing	Formal communications focused on listening, e.g. focus groups Recovery plan enacted by management team – small new beginnings, e.g. small investments, new messages via new communication channels, training etc. Provide space and time to test the new Promote creative thinking Encourage experimentation Avoid punishing mistakes, treat them as learning opportunities Mentoring Praise and publish success Provide feedback
Consolidation	Formal communications focused on dialogue and engagement to explore how to benefit from the new future, e.g. joint working parties Performance targets set as challenging but achievable Review performance and learning Recognise and reward good performance Encourage people to help each other Broadcast successes
Internalisation	Implement new working arrangements arising from joint working parties Review change process and apply new learning for the future Conduct post-implementation reviews

ML4 – Integrated People Strategy

The direction for the company comes from the integrated enterprise strategy, of which the people strategy is part. The enterprise strategy is summarised in the vision and values. Coordination is thus primarily by norms. HR uses the vision and values to inform and guide all of its practices at ML4. The agility of the organisation is facilitated by the 'lattice' structure we discussed in chapter two. The organisation may therefore take on the shape of the network or N-form.

We saw in chapter two that the organisation takes on a flexible structure at ML4. Prior to ML4, organisational units are implicitly treated as if they were of equal status, or, at most, there is merely a distinction between 'line' and 'staff' functions. At ML4, the different organisational units are given distinct assignments, hence different overall accountabilities. A taxonomy for such units is set out in Table 14 (see Goold and Campbell, chapter five).

Table 14. Types of Organisational Units			
Type	*Accountability*	*Explanation*	*Example*
Business unit	To gain competitive advantage in order to deliver bottom-line results from focusing on designated product/ market segments	Prime units for generating profits Substantial autonomy granted by parent unit	UK business unit
Business function	To develop functional expertise to support the success of the business unit	Reports to business unit general manager	Divisional Finance
Overlay unit	To achieve additional commercial benefits through focusing on designated product/ market segments that are not assigned to business units	Acts as a pressure group for the product/ market segment that the conventional business units fail to focus on May refer to parent unit to arbitrate Low autonomy	Global specialist chemical coatings unit where bulk chemical business units are defined by geography
Sub-business	To gain competitive advantage in order to deliver bottom-line results in narrower segments as part of the larger business unit	Reports to business unit general manager Low autonomy	North-west regional unit in the UK business unit
Core resource unit	To develop selected resources, competences or activities into competitive advantage for several business units, and to allocate these resources in line with corporate priorities	Acts as resource provider to other units	Global research and development unit
Shared service unit	To provide services to meet the needs of other units, cost-effectively and responsively	Measured on customer service and unit cost of services Policy set by the parent unit Autonomy over service provision	Global financial 'back office' unit, e.g. accounts payable and accounts receivable

Project unit	To carry out a time-limited, specific, assigned task or project that cuts across several units	Pressure group on behalf of the project	Global project to implement new enterprise resource planning IT system
Parent unit	To carry out obligatory governance tasks and to influence and add value to other units	Overall responsibility for performance and reputation of the whole company Reports to the Board of Directors	Global headquarters
Parent function	To assist the parent unit with specialist skills to meet governance, compliance and due diligence tasks	Reports to senior managers in the parent unit	Shareholder relations office

Over time, a given organisational unit may evolve from one type to another, as business requirements change. So, for example, an overlay unit may transform into a business unit, changing its accountabilities accordingly. To facilitate these changes in unit assignments, senior executives hold formal OE reviews facilitated by HR to ensure structures and roles remain relevant and add value.

As we have discussed already, no one organisational structure solves all coordination problems because a structure is a two-dimensional solution to a multidimensional problem. Thus, HR actively identifies areas of potential conflict and ambiguity that lie between the boxes on the organisation charts – the so-called 'white space'. Liaison devices are designed and implemented as appropriate to manage these residual coordination problems (Mintzberg, p.105). See Table 15 for examples of such devices. It is these liaison devices that reinforce the lattice structure. Such devices may be permanent or temporary, formal or informal, face-to-face or virtual.

Job analysis takes a quantum leap. The focus moves from tasks at ML2, outputs at ML3 to inputs at ML4. The desired knowledge, skills and competencies of the role are identified. Thus, the JD takes one more step change at ML4. At this maturity level, personal development is a prime focus

Table 15. Liaison Devices	
Liaison roles	Unique roles that link the respective departments
Inter-departmental meetings	Permanent or temporary meetings to agree coordinated actions
Task forces	Temporary short-term multifunctional teams assigned a particular problem to resolve
Project teams	A variation on the above but usually more long-term. An individual may be a member of more than one project team. The core membership tends to be permanent, unlike a task force
Integration managers	Appointed as the permanent interface of the structure, e.g. product managers in a departmental structure
Formal coordination systems	Systems that build in the coordination automatically, e.g. an enterprise resource planning system (ERP)

(see chapter eight). The JD thus becomes a Role Profile. Here, the Role Profile describes not only the key results areas (KRA) – the 'what' of the role – but, more importantly, the skills and behavioural competencies – the 'how' of the role. In fact, it is only at this ML that the addition of competencies makes sense. For at this level, the vision and values of the organisation have been proven to add value, are fully understood and accepted. Employees are granted the autonomy to contribute towards the organisation's aims because, and only because, they are aligned to the vision and values. Further, only through the data analysis and cause-effect modelling at ML3 have the competencies that drive added value been identified. We will return to competencies in chapter five when discussing calibre and talent.

We saw in chapter two that coordination at ML4 is enhanced by the formation of SMTs. This also influences job design. Each team requires an array of knowledge, skills and abilities (KSA) in order to accomplish its mission. The members of the team will differ in their level of competency for each specific KSA. These levels of competency can be mapped for each team member onto a skills matrix. The skills matrix in essence becomes the role profile for the whole team. This further demonstrates the dynamic nature of role profiles at ML4, but in stark contrast to the commensurate dynamism at ML1a. As KSA improve, so the skills matrix is updated.

The responsible autonomy characteristic on this ML is supported by practices that facilitate self-managed teams (SMT). Authority levels are reviewed and delegated to the lowest level practicable. Team and meeting processes are adapted to support collegiate involvement.

The combination of the role profiles, skills matrices and SMTs makes each employee an active architect over her own job design. Job crafting is the name given to this phenomenon. Within the broad boundaries set by the firm, each employee is able to construct her own role in terms of tasks, projects, teams, skills and competencies in order to deliver desired results.

The organisation has a stronger sense of partnership with its employees when managing change. Strategy, in its broad sense, is shared and consulted upon. The future implications of strategy for staff are openly debated. Change is now part of the 'day job'. In essence, there are no ends, only means. Change becomes more of a strategic intent and continuous process, rather than mere events. Hence, change messages now cover not just the 'big what', the local detailed 'what' and 'how', but also the 'why' – that is, the strategic imperatives for change. These imperatives are clearly informed by the external monitoring and environmental scanning that is unique to this maturity level.

Thus, where the business intends to enter the public domain with possible future action, it consults on a 'statement of future intent' (SOFI). This is the declaration of the intention to change some critical aspects of the organisation in the distant future. The proposed endgame may be clear, but timescales and details are as yet indeterminate. As details and timescales become clearer, subsequent SOI and SP are made. The change management perspective is now long-term. This completes the range of change management tools. A summary is given in Table 16.

Summary

In this chapter, we have seen how roles and structures shift as an organisation steps through the four maturity levels. At ML1a, structures and roles are dynamic and fluid, morphing to match the daily demands on the business. Change is a constant. No two days are the same. Role clarity comes from the direction of the founder and immediate pressures on the enterprise. It is held together by the founder and her mission. This coherence dissipates at ML1b. The fluidity of ML1a deteriorates into ambiguity. As the founder backs off or even leaves, purpose and context become unclear. The division of labour increases and jobs become ever more vague. Change is erratic. The organisation becomes fragmented and there is no guiding principle to explain the structure.

Table 16. Change Management Tools			
Change Event	*Stage*	*Core Message*	*Description*
Public domain action	The organisation's intent to explore future changes may enter the public domain	Statement of future intent (SOFI)	The declaration of the intent to change some critical aspect of the organisation in the distant future The proposed endgame may be clear, but timescales, details and the likely impact upon employee groups may still be indeterminate or dependent on external factors
Public commitment action	The organisation's intent would lead to an irrevocable public commitment	Statement of intent (SOI)	The confirmation of the intent to change a critical aspect of the organisation in the future The proposed endgame is now firm and the broad impact on employee groups is now clearer, but timescales and details have yet to be determined
Reorganisation action	The intent to make changes within 30-60 days*	Specific proposal (SP)	The proposal to change some critical aspect of the organisation in the near future The endgame, timescales and impact on employee groups are detailed
Post-change action	The consolidation following a critical change event	Recovery process (RP)	The process of recovering from any one of the above change events, so as to bring organisational health, welfare and performance to at least the level achieved prior to that change event

* 30-60 days is based upon the current minimum requirements of legislation in place concerning redundancy proposals in the UK. Other jurisdictions may have different de jure and de facto timescales.

Table 17. Summary – Organisational Effectiveness			
ML	*OML*	*HRML*	
1	Entrepreneurial Management	Initial	a) Direct supervision by founder 　Vision of the founder 　Fluid structure 　Dynamic jobs 　High role ambiguity 　Change as a constant b) Rudimentary management structure 　No 'organising principle' 　Ambiguous job design 　No OD practices 　Erratic change management 　'Mushroom approach'
2	Process Management	Foundational	Direction from and coordination by CEO Organisational functional design: 'organising principle' U-form Organisation charts CEO manages the 'white space' Functional task analysis High vertical and horizontal specialisation Strictly defined and limited authority levels, except for CEO Narrow job design Job description as task inventory Competent management teams Meeting tools PACER Core management responsibilities Basic change management Change as events Specific proposal with social plan Communications pack

3	Proficiency Management	HR Agenda	SBUs M-form SBU/functional strategic agendas Alternating decentralisation/centralisation Organisational design: horizontal and vertical role clarity Delayered organisational structure Hierarchical accountability levels I-VII SLAs Job outcome analysis Role description: RRAA statement Change as punctuated flux with facilitated transitions Intermediate change management Statement of intent
4	Systematic Management	Integrated People Strategy	Vision and values in use Coordination by norms Flexible 'lattice' structure Types of organisational units OE reviews Liaison devices Role profiles Skills matrices SMTs Job crafting Advanced change management Change as an ongoing process Statement of future intent

Order is restored when the organisation shifts to ML2. This is achieved through a rigid functional structure consisting of narrowly defined jobs. Coordination comes from this organisational design and the one general manager. Procedures abound and change management in such a context is, in itself, an SOP.

ML2 is efficient, but only if the environment is stable and the business has merely to manage a steady state. The realisation that standing still is not an option in a changing world may spur the firm to shift to ML3. The strain on the one general manager also acts as a stimulus to reform. SBUs are created and the structure is delayered and roles expand in their remits. Change management is now focused on the medium term.

The limitations of the M-form and the focus purely on KPI-oriented performance (see chapter six) act as a stimulus for the enterprise to move to ML4. The lattice structure enables the firm to flex and adapt as the needs arise. Temporary structures emerge and then fade as required. Roles shift as the occupants develop and as needs change. The apparent return of the ambiguity of ML1b is tolerable as coordination is within SMTs and across the organisation by mission and values. Change is once more a constant – a process rather than a series of events.

The characteristics of OE at the four levels are summarised in Table 17.

CHAPTER 5

CALIBRE & TALENT

Introduction

In the HR strategic framework discussed in chapter three, we have already defined the two sides of C&T as:

- Defining, attracting, acquiring, deploying, progressing and releasing the workforce and
- Creating a critical mass of performance drivers and change agents

- Offering career opportunities and progression

So, this pillar covers workforce planning, employee resourcing and talent management. For many, this is the core process of HR – the employee life cycle. In this chapter, we will explore how HR practices develop as an organisation moves through the four maturity levels. The reader will be able to evaluate the degree to which a firm fulfils the sub-elements of the definition of C&T, set out above in terms of efficiency, effectiveness and motivation at any one level.

ML1 – Initial

There is no systematic workforce planning at this level. The focus is very short-term, so hiring is either to meet the burning needs of expansion or to replace a leaver quickly. The theme is very much one of 'hiring hands'.

The hiring process, in common with all other HR practices at ML1, is ad hoc. No two interviews look the same. Selection is thus almost a random process. Interviews are generally unstructured. A skills interview may be conducted to test whether the applicant can do the job, but immediately. Given the fluid nature of the firm at this level, hiring in the critical skills is the priority. However, what exactly those skills are can vary from month to month. Additionally, job trials may be used – testing the applicant out on the job for a few hours, days or weeks. Early in the existence of the firm, and especially at ML1a, the applicant may also be assessed, casually, for 'team fit'. At ML1a, the overall approach depends upon the 'blueprint' that the founder works from, implicitly or explicitly (see Table 3). As the firm phases into ML1b, the hiring process becomes more haphazard.

Managers claim that they 'know what good looks like' and select accordingly. Halo effects, other biases and discriminations are common at this level. The sporadic approach to recruitment may lead to high turnover, especially for employees with relatively low service.

Employees are deployed as needs arise, being directed to the most urgent requirement on a daily or even hourly basis. Workers may be released as quickly as they are hired.

There is no talent management at ML1. The focus is on immediate outcomes as the future is uncertain. At this level, long-term talent management would be considered an unaffordable luxury. Consequently, in common with all other processes at this ML, employees progress in an ad hoc manner, if at all. Promotions with or without enhanced reward packages take place, but with no apparent rhyme or reason.

The leaders that are sought and found at this ML are of the 'hero' type. As heroic effort is required to achieve virtually anything at this ML, it follows that this leadership model is self-fulfilling and self-perpetuating. Role models arise that reinforce this image, which in turn can lock the organisation at this level for years – if not, managerial generations. Other leadership 'types' are either sidelined or self-select and leave. At this level, 'talent' is implicitly defined as 'heroic'.

ML2 – Foundational

The prime contribution to the business from HR at this ML is systematic staffing and resourcing. This is the dominant theme at this level. The performance of the overall enterprise is advanced most by hiring in talent (Curtis et al, p.30-31).

Thus, the prime HR tool at ML2 is the person specification. This builds upon the JD we discussed in chapter four. The specification sets out the essential and desirable attributes of the ideal candidate for the job. The details in the specification may vary from company to company, but it tends to include at least the following elements – the so-called KSA/E:

- Knowledge/Qualifications
- Skills
- Abilities
- Experience.

The key focus in terms of KSA/E, however, remains *technical* competency.

The overall process of attracting and selecting candidates is mapped out, similar to all other work processes at ML2 – this is, in itself, an SOP. Using the person specification as a template, the central selection tool is the structured interview. The interview is designed to identify candidates who can fulfil the requirements of the job with minimal training. The focus is mainly on technical abilities.

The hiring process, however, cannot commence without due authorisation. This is captured in a suitable document, such as a personnel requisition form (PRF). The level of authority to proceed with hiring may be relatively high up in the organisation as the engagement of an employee is seen as a fixed cost by the business. Control is regarded as the prerogative of senior executives, if not the CEO alone. Due to the rudimentary nature of workforce planning at this maturity level, headcount control can only be managed at the entry and exit stages of the employee life cycle.

Workforce planning is not so much absent as implicit at this ML. It arises as a consequence of other processes, namely: organisational design, job design, rosters and budgets. All of these disparate processes result in the definition of the 'establishment' – the number and types of jobs that can be staffed. All is, however, subject to budgetary constraints. Hence, temporary recruitment freezes are common at this ML. Further, temporary staff may be hired or secured through agencies to meet peak workload or to fill vacancies temporarily.

The new hire's performance is monitored during her first 100 days. This forms the so-called probationary period. Regardless of how sophisticated or simple the assessment process is, it is designed to judge whether the new hire is suitable or not. The underlying critical question that the line manager has to answer is: "Can the new hire do the prescribed job tasks to the required standard?"

Having hired recruits, the firm seeks to secure the effective productivity of the workforce. So, overall, the enterprise endeavours to 'manage time'. Working time is defined by place of work, hours of duty, 'clocking' times, shifts and rosters. Appointment diaries define customer visits, internal and external meetings.

Working time 'anomalies' are also rigorously managed. A time and attendance (T&A) system and an array of policies and procedures facilitate this aspect of C&T. Permissible anomalies such as annual leave are considered, granted and recorded. Sickness is recorded, and return to work (RTW) and rehabilitation procedures are invoked. Lateness and absence without leave (AWOL) are recorded and management action is taken. Persistent absentees may be subject to disciplinary action (see chapter six).

Vacancies are advertised internally, as well as externally. Internal candidates may apply for positions using the internal appointments SOP. However, the specification for jobs is the same for both internal and external candidates. As the hierarchy is deep and authority levels limited, except for the most senior roles, promotions tend to be administrative promotions only. That is, the successful candidate may get a higher grade and a larger reward package, but this comes with little in the way of broader responsibilities or decision-making authority.

To manage the release of employees, a range of exit procedures are in place. These cover all types of voluntary and involuntary leavers.

Conceptually, overall talent management is about calibre acquisition, retention, development and exit: CARDE for short. The emphasis on each component element of this acronym varies at each of the maturity levels. As we have already stated, resourcing is the prime focus at ML2. In addition, there is always the need to churn calibre that does not meet performance expectations. Hence, talent management could be summarised as CArdE at this maturity level – that is, with the emphasis on acquisition and exit. As we have seen, calibre at ML2 is essentially defined in terms of technical expertise.

Talent management is basic at ML2. Its main focus is on replacement planning. The calibre agenda is a closed process – that is, it is conducted by the senior management team only (or even just the CEO and VP, HR) and is not disclosed to the wider organisation. Critical calibre roles are defined and potential successors identified. These roles tend to be the most senior jobs in the organisation, with a few highly technical roles added to the analysis. Critical calibre roles are those that are expected to give maximum leverage to organisational performance. As we have seen, the chances are that any replacement for these roles could be an outside hire.

However, some high potential employees (HIPOs) may be identified by this process. The firm will work to the principle of 'top talent for top jobs'. Simply identifying HIPOs and potential replacements for executives at this maturity level is felt to be sufficient. Few, if any, talent management actions are undertaken. In actuality, the talent management processes and the internal appointment process do not connect at this ML. So, even where a HIPO is identified, this does not influence the appointment, even when a suitable vacancy arises.

As can be imagined, this form of talent management does not take too much time. It is more of a risk analysis or human capital 'stock check'.

ML3 – HR Agenda

The degree of sophistication under this pillar of the HR strategic framework takes a quantum leap at this maturity level. As we saw in chapter two, under proficiency management, strategic plans arise at ML3 – at the enterprise, the SBU and the functional levels. However, as has already been discussed, for the vast majority of employees, the organisation is still functional in nature.

Each SBU now conducts a medium-term functional workforce planning process. Derived from the SBU strategy, a workforce plan is devised to support that strategy. Expansions and contractions of the workforce, the skill mix, the churn rates, and internal promotion rates are all factored into this planning. In essence, workforce planning aims to assess the demand for and the supply of labour and skills in the medium term and then to put in place actions to close any perceived gaps between demand and supply. Forecasting in this area is notoriously difficult and any apparent precision may be, to a great extent, spurious. However, the key element here is that the enterprise consciously addresses this form of planning in a proactive manner rather than the reactive approach at ML2.

The firm also adopts a competency framework or, more accurately, frameworks. Job families are still defined along functional lines, so the frameworks follow suit. As little analysis is yet possible, these competency frameworks are taken 'off the shelf' rather than being designed bespoke. The organisation has limited data, at least at the start of ML3, to define what 'good' looks like. Hence, energy is best focused on building up experience of competencies in general rather than conducting full-blown job/competency analysis tailored to the firm.

The competency frameworks inform and expand person specifications and selection techniques. Hence competency-based interviewing, psychometric tests, personality questionnaires and assessment centres can be more effectively designed and implemented at this maturity level.

As with the new hire at ML2, the line manager assesses him during the probationary period. However, in line with the prime theme at ML3, the key implicit question is: "Will the new hire deliver the numbers?"

Deployment is similar to ML2 but is supplemented in a few ways. As we will see, promotions are difficult to fulfil at ML3 due to the delayered structure. The organisation attempts to circumvent these difficulties by managing job rotations and secondments for HIPOs identified in the talent management processes (see below).

The emphasis in talent management shifts at ML3 towards CARde. That is, the focus is on acquisition *and* retention. Calibre is still hired in for reasons we will explain below, but more energy is now focused on retention. The structure, as we saw in chapter two, is heavily delayered at ML3. This makes the steps between organisational levels big ones. In such circumstances, it is hard to grow talent that can make the leap from a lower level to the next higher managerial level. However, some internal candidates will show promise and be treated as HIPOs accordingly. In line with the characteristics of this ML, calibre is defined in terms of performance delivery, now and potential for the future – literally delivering the numbers.

Hence, talent management tools are developed to identify such top calibre. Firstly, the job family competency frameworks and the delayered organisational structure aid the construction of career ladders, again these are functional ones. These ladders provide a measure of the capability required at each managerial level, in each technical function and are thus a means of assessing potential. Hence, a leadership model starts to emerge at this ML, but it is still a functional version.

Secondly, calibre review boards (CRB) are set up. There are three levels of CRBs: the top team of each divisional function; the SBU executive teams; and the CEO's top team. Each CRB carries out an annual calibre review. The overall process is guided by the HR talent management team. Each manager is rated in terms of performance and potential. A suitable set of rating scales are set out in Tables 18 and 19.

Table 18. Calibre – Potential Ratings	
Rating	*Definition*
A	Consistently demonstrates the potential and competence for step-change* progression within or outside present function
B	Consistently demonstrates the potential and competence for progression within or outside current function
C	Reached own level of competence Competent, or capable of becoming competent at current organisational level
D	No potential demonstrated. Demonstrates lack of competence at current level Progressed beyond own level of competence

* Step-change progression is defined as progress by two promotional steps or more

Table 19. Calibre – Performance Ratings	
Rating	*Definition*
5	Consistently performs well beyond the requirements of the role Performance exceeds expectations
4	Sometimes performs beyond the requirements of the role Performance occasionally exceeds expectation
3	Performance meets the requirements of the role Performs as expected
2	Performance meets some of the requirements of the role, but not all Performs adequately
1	Consistent failure to perform – does not meet the requirements of the role

The combination of potential and performance describes the calibre profile matrix. This is set out in Table 20. Each employee assessed can be placed in this grid. Many organisations use a nine-box grid to display the calibre profile of their internal populations.

'Foundational calibre' is the backbone of the organisation. Most standard people management practices, e.g. performance management, rewards, employee development etc., meet the needs of this population. In fact, these standard practices should be designed to meet the needs of this population.

Table 20. Calibre Profile Matrix

		Potential			
		A	B	C	D
Performance	5	'Rising Stars'		'Foundational Calibre'	n/a
	4				
	3				
	2	'Calibre Enigmas'		'Performance Problems'	'Calibre Problems'
	1				

Table 21. Calibre Actions

Calibre Category	Possible Calibre Actions
'Rising Stars'	Salary tracking Tailored individual development actions (IDA)
'Calibre Enigmas'	Career and/or performance counselling
'Calibre Problems'	Performance counselling Reassignments Calibre exit as a 'casualty of change'
'Calibre Gaps'	Seedcorn recruitment
'Foundational Calibre'	Standard HR practices apply No specific calibre actions required

According to the calibre category that each manager is assigned to, specific calibre actions are agreed by the CRBs. The talent management team tracks these calibre actions to ensure they are implemented appropriately. These are captured as individual career plans (ICP) for those rated as calibre – high or low. A set of general calibre actions are set out in Table 21. These are bespoke to each individual as the standard people management practices (see above) are not sufficiently tailored. For example, 'salary tracking' is designed to keep the individual's reward package competitive in the market. In essence, each calibre action is designed to demonstrate that the firm values the individual as 'talent'.

This calibre review process then enables medium-term succession planning to be systematically carried out. Potential successors can be identified for managerial levels within each function. Calibre gaps can also be spotted where external hires may still be necessary or where more creative internal development may be required. Hence, at ML3, talent management is proactive.

ML4 – Integrated People Strategy

This level has the overriding theme of the 'strategic competency agenda'. Derived from the experience built up at ML3 and the vision and values created at ML4, the organisation can define and prove its own competency framework. This framework is tested by the detailed analysis that is conducted once ML3 is fully implemented and has run for some time. Those competencies that drive performance and reflect the core competence of the organisation are those that are validated and selected for the strategic competency framework at ML4. This informs all other aspects of the people strategy at this maturity level.

As with other aspects at ML4, there is an integrated workforce plan. This is defined not just in terms of numbers, but in terms of skills and competencies. As we saw in chapter two, only the core workforce, and those roles that are complementary to this core, are retained as direct employees by the organisation. Hence, part of the integrated workforce plan includes the outsourcing of ancillary work and workers.

Recruitment and selection is still competency-based, but founded on the strategic framework. Selection tools are adapted to suit. The cultural values are key factors in selection to ensure any new hire has a good 'cultural fit'.

New hires still go through a probationary period. The intrinsic questions at ML4 are: "Is the new hire a 'good fit' with our culture? Will she develop further?"

Employees are deployed not only to utilise their skills, but also to develop their KSA further. This forms part of the career development experiences (CDE) that we will cover in chapter eight.

In line with the design of roles at this ML (see chapter four), employees progress horizontally and vertically. Climbing the career ladder is not the only way to progress at ML4. Horizontally, the employee expands the skills at his current organisational level, ultimately developing mastery. Greater responsibilities give vertical progression. This may be by way of delegated authority (job enrichment) or through promotion. However, unlike at ML2, the specification for internal candidates is different from that for external candidates. Internal applicants have to demonstrate *aptitude* for the higher level. External candidates have to demonstrate *competency*, i.e. they already have the skills for the role *and* that they are a good cultural fit.

The enterprise aims to avoid unnecessary exits. The investment in employees is high at ML4. To dismiss an employee is a poor return on that investment. Thus, the prime aim is to retain and reform any poor performer, especially those with longer tenure.

The talent agenda now embraces all employees. This is because only the core workforce is employed directly by the business *and* their skills are central to the value-creation process in and of the business. Hence, investment in this workforce has a proven return for enterprise value-creation. So, calibre is now defined in terms of the strategic competencies across the whole workforce. The shape of the calibre agenda also changes. It now looks like: CaRDe. That is, the predominant focus is on retention and development. The talent management, appointment processes, training & development interventions and employee deployment processes are now an integrated whole, all focused on raising capability.

Career ladders still exist, but more as a latticed frame to guide the creation of individual career maps. The team-orientation of the company lends itself to more lateral and diagonal career moves rather than just the traditional vertical moves.

Calibre is rated in a similar manner to the tools used at ML3, but with the addition of a leadership metric and the change from performance to a contribution rating. As change is a constant in this agile organisation, the adaptability of each individual is a key measure. This is assessed, for example, using the additional ratings as set out in Table 22.

The performance rating scale is replaced by that of 'contribution'. This is a more long-term view of the individual's impact than that assessed at ML3. The focus at ML3 was on delivery of the numbers, usually with a time horizon of no greater than a year. At ML4, the focus shifts to a longer-term appraisal of the individual, covering competency, teamwork, coaching etc. as well as outputs.

The calibre reviews introduced in ML3 continue to identify talent pools at the different organisational levels via the CRB process.

Calibre actions are similar to those set out under ML3. In addition, calibre opportunities are more readily created at ML4. The fluid nature of the organisational structure at this level, and the team orientation, enable more development opportunities to be designed.

All employees now have ICPs. This is strongly competency-based. Thus, the overall calibre agenda is open – that is, each employee is fully aware of her ratings and development plans. It is a transparent process.

Table 22. Calibre – Leadership Ratings		
Rating	*Title*	*Definition*
L	'Pioneer'	Leads others in identifying and implementing sustainable step-change initiatives in line with the business 'big picture' A pioneer and change agent. Inspires others to change
I	'Improver'	Contributes ideas and suggestions effectively to step-change initiatives Implements and actively supports change
M	'Implementer'	Effective at carrying out change initiatives primarily designed by others Often takes a task leadership role. Sees such change through to completion Tends to wait for the call from others
F	'Follower'	Prefers the status quo Cooperates with initiatives when prompted Neutral on change, as such
B	'Preserver'	Actively preserves the 'way we do things around here' Prevents or blocks change, actively or covertly Holds the business back

Summary

The elements of C&T through the four maturity levels are summarised in Table 23.

In this chapter, we have described the evolution of techniques under C&T as a firm progresses through the maturity levels. At ML1, processes and practices are ad hoc. As we will see in chapter eight, there is little or no systematic training at this ML. Consequently, there is a need for immediate skills. Employees have to hit the ground running. Often businesses at ML1 face a chronic shortage of skilled labour. There is no talent management. This is partially due to the lack of a formal organisational structure to develop in and partially due to the short-term nature of the operation. The implicit model of 'talent' is the heroic one. As we have seen, little gets accomplished at ML1 other than through heroic effort. There is no workforce planning as the firm has no plans as such, anyway. Any career progression is for 'heroes' or by leaving the business altogether, hence the dire retention issues faced by the enterprise at this level.

As with other pillars of the HR strategic framework, a sense of order is restored at ML2, but in a rigid manner. We have seen that systematic staffing and

ML	OML	HRML	
**Table 23. Summary – Calibre & Talent**			

ML	OML	HRML	
1	Entrepreneurial Management	Initial	No workforce planning (WFP) 'Hiring hands' Ad hoc resourcing Hire in critical skills Unstructured or skills interview Job trials Halo effects and other biases No talent management (TM) 'Hero' model of leadership
2	Process Management	Foundational	Establishment as WFP Systematic staffing and resourcing Person specification KSA/E Technical ability Structured interview PRF 'Managing time' Working time and related anomalies Attendance management Time & attendance systems RTW interview Closed calibre agenda CArdE HIPOs identified Replacement planning Critical calibre roles Passive TM
3	Proficiency Management	HR Agenda	Medium-term SBU/functional WFP Functional competency frameworks (off-the-shelf) CBI Psychometrics CARde Career ladders Calibre review boards Calibre ratings: performance and potential Calibre profile matrix

			CRB Succession plans Calibre gaps Calibre actions ICP for 'high calibre' Emergent leadership models Proactive TM
4	Systematic Management	Integrated People Strategy	Strategic competency agenda Integrated WFP and TM Validated strategic competency framework CaRDe Different internal and external selection criteria Career maps Calibre ratings: contribution, potential, and leadership Talent pools Creating calibre opportunities ICP for all

resourcing is the key theme at this level. Hiring in talent has the greatest effect upon productivity at ML2. The basic practices of recruitment are characteristic of HRML2, all centred on supporting the structured interview. Basic talent management emerges at ML2. This focuses on replacement management, critical calibre roles and high potential staff. Workforce planning is rudimentary.

At ML3, functional competencies arise. The competency frameworks are usually off-the-shelf. Selection techniques thus become more sophisticated. Along with these frameworks, the delayered organisational structure at one and the same time facilitates and hinders a more comprehensive approach to talent management. The calibre agenda shifts to acquisition and retention. Workforce planning is, as with most planning at ML3, medium-term and functional in nature.

At ML4, C&T guides all other pillars of the HR strategic framework. The identification of core competences and the development of the derived strategic competency framework inform all other HR practices. Workforce planning is fully integrated and the calibre agenda is fully open.

CHAPTER 6

PERFORMANCE MANAGEMENT SYSTEMS

Introduction

In the HR strategic framework, we defined PMS as:

- Deploying organisational intent,
- Regulating individual behaviour and
- Holding employees accountable
- Creating an environment in which each employee can succeed

In this chapter, we will examine how an enterprise attempts to align its employees' efforts with the organisation's will, in order to deliver the desired behaviours and results. We will see how the focus of the PMS shifts as the firm moves through the four maturity levels.

ML1 – Initial

In the start-up phase (ML1a), the implicit intent of the organisation is to 'make and sell' in order to survive and grow. Employees concentrate on delivering immediate outputs. Accountabilities are tacit and shift from day-to-day. Employees just get on with it. Feedback tends to be immediate and based upon direct observation by the founder or by co-workers. In fact, regulation is often via peer pressure. There are no formal systems, processes or forms that could be described as conventional performance management, as such.

As the business shifts into the emergent phase (ML1b), more formal accountancy controls emerge. The implicit intent and prime measure is budgetary delivery. This provides a measure on an annual, quarterly and monthly basis. However, for most employees, time horizons tend to be much shorter. The budget may carry the label annual operating plan (AOP), though this is not so much a plan as a commitment or aspiration. Depending upon the department or managerial job, the budget may be expressed in terms of revenue, cost, cash flow or profit. In reality, the PMS is embedded in, and limited to and by the financial reporting system. The only goals set are financial goals. Hence, below the levels of revenue centre and cost centre, performance management in any formal sense is effectively absent. For most employees, there are no goals.

Accountabilities other than financial are thus not measured on any systematic basis, except when something 'goes wrong'. This reflects the 'compliance' culture that is characteristic of ML1b. So, from time to time, other PMS concerns arise. These ad hoc requirements occur because of the limitations of the financial reporting system. Finances on their own are incapable of providing sufficient monitoring and control of even a relatively small enterprise, let alone a large one. So, to meet these ad hoc requirements, separate reports are demanded and created. A range of disparate reports therefore arises. Many linger on as legacy systems long after the immediate need for them has expired. Thus, the PMS builds up initially around the financial system, but with an ever-widening range of 'bolt on' reports covering various other diverse issues. Thus, the PMS becomes highly fragmented in nature.

For the vast majority of employees, there is no PMS as such. Individual performance management applies only to budget holders. For the rest, the PMS is ad hoc. Only if things go wrong is there any feedback and so this is almost always negative. Compliance errors are corrected, if they are detected at all. The lack of effective monitoring systems means that mistakes may remain hidden. Thus, poor performance may be tacitly tolerated by neglect for years. There are no formal codes of conduct. However, managers may attempt to correct what they regard as bad behaviour. Due to inconsistencies, this tends to come across as regulation through managerial idiosyncrasy.

Rudimentary disciplinary action, formal and informal, arises at ML1b. However, as there is poor monitoring and there is no systematic management of individual performance, low level, early counselling and disciplinary action does not take place. Such action is not considered part of a manager's job at this ML. Thus, performance problems 'suddenly' arise. Performance may 'suddenly' be deemed to be unacceptable and the individual is then dealt with summarily. Thus, dismissal may be the only means used to manage substandard performance. However, as dismissal is seen as an extreme act, the poor performance may be tolerated for some time, until a gross error is made and management can 'stand it' no longer. The lack of monitoring and feedback systems also means that the individual is unlikely to be aware of his underperformance and the opportunity to self-correct goes begging.

ML2 – Foundational

The intent of the organisation is still implicit at this maturity level: stability and efficiency. We will see below how the organisation communicates this intent, but by indirect means.

As we saw in chapter four on Organisational Effectiveness, each employee now has a clear definition of her duties captured in the job description. The job is relatively narrow in terms of design. In addition, the SOPs highlight each person's tasks in fine detail. Personal conduct is prescribed in, and proscribed by codes of conduct and statements of minimum standards of performance (MSOP). Broader disciplinary offences are set out in the relevant disciplinary procedures. Thus, organisational intent is implicit and embedded in the job design, SOPs and short-term work schedules.

For the management population, there is a Management by Objectives (MbO) annual cascade process. SMART goals are set for managers and other target-driven employees, e.g. sales staff. The definition of SMART varies from textbook to textbook, but below is a common set:

- Specific – precisely defined
- Measurable – quantitatively
- Achievable
- Relevant – to the job and to the aims of the business
- Time-trackable – progress can be monitored and measured on a regular basis.

SMART goals may also be divided into common themes, e.g. financial, operational, projects, personal. However, in line with the structures at ML2, they are exclusively functionally oriented. Occasionally, the organisation will mandate company-wide initiatives through the SMART goals, e.g. safety.

There is an annual appraisal cycle. At the start of the year, goals are set. A mid-year review (MYR) is then held. A full-year review (FYR) is finally conducted. The timetable tends to mirror the financial reporting cycle. However, this appraisal cycle is still regarded as a 'bolt-on' to the real budgetary review process, which follows a shorter cycle time, monthly if not weekly or even daily. The appraisal form serves multiple purposes and is generally a combined performance and development review (PADR). Hence, personal development goals are treated on an equal footing to performance goals. However, this combined approach tends to crowd out most of the developmental aims of the system.

Overall, the PMS remains fragmented at ML2. It is better to talk of systems rather than a single performance management system. The various procedures and systems in the enterprise mean that there are multiple sets of SOPs, standards and targets – financial, operational, quality, compliance, IT etc. Few of these will actually be captured in the HR-prescribed appraisal process. In fact, if all of these performance systems were incorporated into the appraisal process, they would overload it.

Partly because of this disparate set of performance systems, managers, in particular, have to submit regular reports on a wide range of topics. These are themselves part of the nexus that constitutes the performance management systems. Virtually all of these reports convey 'no news'.

Operational staff will tend not to have appraisals. The nature of their jobs at this ML is such that goal-setting serves no great purpose. If they do have an annual appraisal, the focus is on 'duties done' and how they could improve in their jobs. However, as operational staff are required to abide by the SOP, improvements are hard to identify. Hence, for operational staff, any appraisal actually conducted tends to be ritualistic at best. Enforcement of appraisals at this operational level tends to be problematic, as even first line managers cannot see the point of imposing them upon their subordinates.

Projects are tracked in monthly management meetings. While projects may be captured in a person's SMART goals, reviewing them on a six-monthly basis (at MYR and FYR) is inadequate for project management. Hence, projects are reviewed in monthly management meetings, but on an ad hoc basis.

Sales staff are issued with sales incentive plans (SIP). These specify the targets, usually on a monthly basis, that each sales person has to hit. The SIP is a breakdown of the overall sales budget for the business as a whole. There are normally 3-5 specific metrics, e.g. revenue, gross margin, profit, cash etc. The SIP links directly to the sales incentive bonus (SIB) that we will return to when discussing reward and recognition in chapter nine.

Other than the SIB, there are only tenuous links between performance and other rewards. For example, managers may participate in a management bonus scheme. This, however, tends to be a variation on profit-share and not linked to individual performance, as such a link would be spurious at this maturity level. Under such a scheme, a given percentage of salary is paid out annually to all participating according to the profit performance of their business unit. Only in the case of very poor performance would the bonus be withheld or reduced. This is, however, rare (see chapter nine).

In cases of poor performance, an employee is put on a performance improvement plan (PIP). This procedure is documented and review meetings are held regularly until performance returns to an acceptable level or until disciplinary action is invoked. The disciplinary procedure is also clearly documented, as are any individual disciplinary proceedings. In some jurisdictions, this is a statutory requirement or necessary to build an audit trail to support the case in any subsequent legal action. At ML2, the disciplinary procedure is a detailed process in its own right and part of the broader performance management systems.

ML3 – HR Agenda

Performance delivery and continuous improvement (CI) are the dominant themes at ML3. We saw in chapter two that ML3 is characterised by a multitude of short-interval measurements. Key performance indicators (KPI) for input, process and output measures pervade the whole of the organisation. All business units and individuals have associated input, process and/or output targets and supportive CI plans. KPIs are thus endemic and evident throughout the whole business. The firm uses communication devices, such as visual management, that tell "… at a glance how work should be done and whether it deviates from the standard." (Liker, 2004, p.152).

Thus, the intent of the organisation, or rather of the SBU and functions, is clearly apparent to all employees. The strategy of each SBU and its functions will be conveyed in general, through communication channels (see chapter seven), and then specifically to each individual through her role description and the PMS itself. The intent of the overall enterprise is, however, less evident to most employees. Where the HQ delegates authority to the SBUs, only the financial targets convey the enterprise's intent. As at ML1b, financials are poor communication devices as they lack 'richness' (see chapter seven).

The KPIs are rolled up into functional, SBU and organisational balanced scorecards (BSC) or similar dashboard displays. However, the SBU BSC is operational in nature as it is an accumulation of the detailed functional KPIs and not derived from any business-wide strategy (see ML4 below). The overall enterprise simply focuses on a summary dashboard consisting of the limited financial targets it sets the SBUs.

The BSCs are used to track progress versus target. Where an actual outcome deviates from target, this is colour-coded on a 'CRAGS' basis (see Table 24).

Table 24. 'CRAGS' Performance Model – Balanced Scorecard		
Code	Performance Level	Definition
S	'Silver'	Where a KPI's performance significantly exceeds target
G	'Green'	Where a KPI's performance meets or exceeds target
A	'Amber'	Where a KPI's performance falls marginally below target
R	'Red'	Where a KPI's performance falls significantly below target
C	'Crimson'	Where a KPI's performance falls seriously below target

Reporting on performance follows a strict closed-loop performance cycle based upon the 'management by exception' principle (MBE). Only when a measure is out of tolerance or off-track does it enter this cycle. In such circumstances, a variance to target (VTT) is registered. The function accountable for the measure is then required to conduct a root-cause analysis (RCA) to identify the underlying reasons for the adverse variance. The function(s) accountable for the root causes are then required to propose a corrective action plan (CAP) to bring the measure back on track. How well the CAP closes the gap is assessed in terms of a measure of effectiveness (MoE) of the original performance and of the CAP.

The checklist set out in Table 25 summarises the closed-loop performance cycle. Through the BSC and this MBE principle, the organisation is able to cope with much more data than at ML2, but without the panoply of reports characteristic of that specific maturity level. Reports are only required when there is some 'news' to convey, i.e. an exception.

	Table 25. Closed-loop Performance Cycle		
	Stage	*Code*	*Comments*
1	Variance to target	VTT	Is the project on plan? Is the KPI on target?
2	Root-cause analysis	RCA	If the variance is adverse, what are the root causes of this adverse variance? Who is accountable for these root causes?
3	Corrective action plan	CAP	What action can the person accountable take to bring the measure back on plan and/or target? If the RCA suggests that the CAP needs to be carried out under a different accountability, what action can the relevant person take to bring the measure back on plan and/or target?
4	Measure of effectiveness	MoE	Was the person accountable effective in delivering the accountability? Was the CAP effective in bringing the accountability back on plan and/or on target?

We saw when discussing organisational effectiveness (see chapter four) how role accountabilities are more precisely captured in a role, responsibility, authority and accountability statement (RRAA) (see Table 12). This OE tool feeds the corresponding PMS tools. An individual accountability review (IAR) sets out how each accountability will be measured and what the specific target will be for the forthcoming performance period, usually for the next year. Then, it sets out the projects that are needed to deliver these targets and the milestone plans that will enable those projects to be tracked. The IAR is discussed and agreed with the employee's immediate manager, usually for the forthcoming year. The IAR enables a precise definition of performance. A model for an IAR is set out in Table 26.

Table 26. Individual Accountability Review			
Name:	*Role Title:*		*Date:*
Accountability	Measures	Targets	Projects
In this accountability area, what does the organisation hold the occupant accountable for?	For each accountability, how will delivery be measured?	In this review/ budget period, what is the target that will prove the required delivery?	To deliver each target, what improvement projects are needed? For each project, what is the milestone plan?

Thus, each employee can be assessed in terms of the delivery of the KPIs themselves *and* whether she is on-time, in-full (OTIF) to the agreed project milestone plans. This is tracked and captured in an individual contribution report (ICR). A model is described in Table 27. The ICR allows progress to be recorded on an ongoing basis and for this to be rolled-up for quarterly and then the annual review. We will see in chapter nine how the rating of effectiveness is used to apportion rewards.

Table 27. Individual Contribution Report					
Name:		*Title:*		*Date/Period:*	
Area of Accountability	VTT	RCA	CAP	Review Date	MoE
Title of the Area (see RRAA)	How is this accountability measured?				How effective was the original delivery?
	Is it on track or adverse?	Why is it adverse?	What will you do to bring the measure back on track/target?	When and how will the corrective action be reviewed and by whom?	How effective was the corrective action?
	Is the project OTIF to the agreed plan?		What actions will bring the project back on track?		

At ML3, the PMS becomes a part of the organisation's DNA. It is a fully integrated routine of management on a short-interval basis. To support this, each employee has a monthly 1-2-1 meeting with her immediate manager to review progress and agree any corrective action that may be necessary. The focus of the discussion is on delivering – that is, delivery of targets and project milestones. Actual outcomes are recorded on a monthly basis, which rolls up into quarterly and annual reviews. Hence, the 'no surprise' principle applies to individual performance. This is in contrast to ML1 and even ML2. With no discussion or with infrequent meetings on performance at these lower maturity levels, the annual appraisal can come as a shock to the individual who may not have picked up on the fact that his delivery was below par.

Targets at ML3 tend to be 'stretch' targets. The experience of SMART goals at ML2 teaches managers and employees that these are relatively safe goals. This fits with the ethos of ML2, which is primarily concerned with conformance to SOP. Ambitious performance is an outlier at such a maturity level and can even disrupt the stability sought at ML2. At ML3, though, the comprehensive measurement systems and the detailed project management enables the organisation to be bolder. Stretch goals have been defined as targets that have a 50/50 probability of attainment given current capabilities. That is, they demand a leap into the unknown, the invention of new practices, and the acquisition of new skills and/or knowledge. This prepares the organisation for the shift to a competency-based PMS that we will discuss in the next section on ML4.

The performance appraisal process is now separated from the personal development process. That is, the PADR introduced at ML2 is now 'deconstructed'. This avoids the crowding-out effect we touched on when discussing ML2. Where the same process endeavours to have performance *and* development goals, the former crowd out the latter. This conflict is partially resolved by having two distinct processes. We will discuss development goals in chapter eight.

The PIP process that emerged at ML2 evolves into a more sophisticated scheme at ML3. The PIP process at ML2 assumes that one size fits all. However, substandard performance and conduct are not uniform. Marginally substandard performance warrants a completely different approach and a different kind of conversation to critically substandard delivery. Hence, the 'CRAGS' model is applied on an individual basis to the PIP. An example is set out in Table 28.

As the focus at ML3 is on continuous improvement, the aim of PIP is first and foremost to return the employee to acceptable performance as quickly as possible. Thus, the organisation invests in turning around underperformers, even if this entails redeployment to a more suitable role. So, the assumption underlying the 'amber' track in CRAGS (see Table 29) is that the employee's performance can be turned round. It is only in the more critical tracks such as 'crimson' that urgent action on the part of the employee is needed to avoid dismissal. Hence, critical underperformance is fast-tracked, as illustrated in Table 29.

Table 28. 'CRAGS' Performance Improvement Plan					
Code	Performance Level	Definition	Example Guidelines	Management Action Sequence	Ultimate Consequence
S	'Silver'	Where an employee's performance significantly exceeds target	Over 105% of target	Feedback Praise Over-target bonus Continue to monitor	Reward Retain
G	'Green'	Where an employee's performance meets or exceeds target	95 – 105% of target	Thanks Standard bonus Continue to monitor	Recognise Retain
A	'Amber'	Where an employee's performance falls marginally below target	90 – 95% of target	Express support Agree CAP If no improvement, PIP, then standard track disciplinary action	Reform
R	'Red'	Where an employee's performance falls significantly below target	80 – 90% of target	Raise concern and awareness PIP If no improvement, fast-track disciplinary action	Reform Reassign
C	'Crimson'	Where an employee's performance falls seriously below target	Less than 80% of target	Raise alarm Formal warning PIP If no improvement, rapid-track disciplinary action	Replace

Table 29. Disciplinary Procedure Performance Improvement Plan Tracks			
Performance Level	*'Amber'*	*'Red'*	*'Crimson'*
Stages	Standard Track	Fast Track	Rapid Track
I	CAP	PIP	First warning PIP
II	PIP	First warning PIP	Final warning PIP
III	First warning PIP	Final warning PIP	Dismissal
IV	Second warning PIP	Dismissal	
V	Final warning PIP		
VI	Dismissal		

The focus upon CI at ML3 requires investment in a programme management office (PMO). The SBU and functional programmes and projects are tracked by the PMO on behalf of the GMs and their functional heads of department. Formal programme management boards sit to review projects and programmes on a monthly basis. Projects are flagged on a similar colour-coded system to CRAGS (see Table 24).

The programme review boards facilitated by the staff from PMO reflect a tendency to establish focused management meetings at ML3. Each management team now has pre-planned separate monthly meetings on performance and on programmes. In addition, top teams have distinct strategic review sessions on a less frequent basis to evaluate the efficacy of their plans. These separate, focused meetings contrast with the 'one size fits all' management meetings at ML2. In such potpourri meetings, the urgent crowds out the important, the short term crowds out the long.

The link to rewards is much more explicit at ML3 than at lower maturity levels. Individual performance feeds the reward systems, as we shall see in chapter nine. As the organisation has a much more sophisticated measurement system that can gauge the performance of virtually each individual and certainly each manager, this informs individual reward decisions.

All of the tools and practices outlined in this section can be captured in the themes that run throughout this maturity level: 'expectations management' and 'management by consequence'. The RRAA, IAR and ICR spell out the expectations. The six R's spell out management by consequence. These are set out in Table 30. Expectations in terms of delivery and conduct are crystal clear at ML3. Further, outstanding individual performance is rewarded, and poor performance is corrected and/or punished. The message is that 'performance counts' at ML3.

Table 30. Management by Consequence	
Consequence	*Definition*
Reward	The crediting of outstanding contribution through the award of tangible gains to the employee, e.g. a salary rise, bonus payment, promotion etc.
Recognise (with symbol)	The positive appreciation of the employee's exceptional contribution with a formal symbolic element, e.g. a gift, letter, prize, certificate etc.
Recognise (without symbol)	The positive appreciation of the employee's contribution without a formal symbolic element, e.g. verbal praise or thank you This praise may be done in public or in private
Retain	The general acknowledgement of the employee's contribution and the continued engagement of the employee in his current role
Reform	The endeavour to modify the employee's behaviour and/or performance through, e.g. counselling, training etc.
Replace	The removal of the employee from his current role and replacement of him by the appointment of a more suitable candidate The employee may be reassigned, demoted or dismissed

ML4 – Integrated People Strategy

Intent is now fully transparent at this maturity level. There is an explicit integrated enterprise strategy that lays out the long-term direction of the business and converts this into a cohesive portfolio of programmes and projects. This enables a true enterprise performance management system (EPM) to operate. The guardianship of this becomes the overall responsibility of the office for strategic management (OSM), which takes on a wider remit than the PMO associated with ML3. The firm can therefore define those KPIs that will track progress towards its strategic goals. These become strategic key performance indicators (SKPI). Parsimony applies here. The plethora of operational KPIs at ML3 is reduced to a handful of SKPIs at ML4.

Hence, the BSC becomes a truly *strategic* balanced scorecard at ML4 for the enterprise as a whole. These SKPIs are systematically cascaded throughout the organisation, so governing alignment down to the business unit, team and individual levels. Targets are informed by external benchmarking to set world-class aspirations and standards.

Targets are also informed by 360-degree expectations or, more technically, the 'expectations approach' (see Machin). As we saw in chapter four, the organisational structure is no longer purely functional and has evolved into a flexible, lattice structure. Internal customers can now input to the target-setting process. These mutual expectations of internal customer and supplier are discussed and defined. These are captured in the EPM/PMS, which is now a real-time system. This enables a higher degree of self-monitoring by each employee.

1-2-1 meetings have more of a developmental emphasis at ML4. The strategic competency framework has been proven to lead to improved performance. So weight is placed more on developing these rather than addressing performance *directly*. These are less performance reviews and more focused contribution conversations or 'check-ins'. To ensure focus, an annual conversation calendar is established. Tools are devised to support the different conversations, e.g. model agendas, guidelines on style, apps etc. An example of an annual conversation calendar is set out in Table 31, although check-ins may take place as frequently as every week.

Table 31. Annual Contribution Conversation Calendar			
January	Q4/Annual Contribution Discussion	July	Q2 Contribution Discussion
February	Competency Discussion	August	Career and Competency Discussion
March	Performance Discussion	September	Performance Discussion
April	Q1 Contribution Discussion	October	Q3 Contribution Discussion
May	Performance Discussion	November	Performance Discussion
June	Performance Discussion	December	Annual Contribution Agreement/ Re-contracting

We will leave the description of the competency and career discussions for when we cover employee development in chapter eight. Here, the frequency of the different discussions relates to the time taken to change the different subjects under discussion. Careers move slowest, hence only one planned discussion a year. Competencies change a little quicker, hence two sessions a year. Contribution is discussed quarterly, while performance itself changes the most frequently, so five sessions a year. However, the overall focus of the appraisal process is more on 'being and becoming' more competent in terms of the strategic competencies, rather than 'delivering the numbers', as it is at ML3, or 'doing' duties in ML2. Competency at ML4 is effectively a surrogate measure of mastery and organisational citizenship.

Thus, goals and targets now shift more towards *learning* goals. The experience of stretch targets at ML3 and the proof that the strategic competencies lead to future improved performance mean that the organisation can confidently focus on raising individual and team capabilities – performance follows. At lower maturity levels, there was no proven model that would assure the firm that current capabilities lead to enhanced future performance outcomes. At ML4, the business has such a model, hence the full shift to learning rather than 'performance' goals.

The reliance on vision, values and competency means that the company increasingly depends upon normative controls rather than discipline, rules, procedures and detailed comprehensive measurements. Culture now becomes a means of self-monitoring, self-discipline and self-control at ML4. In addition, the formation of SMTs adds the self-discipline of peer pressure.

Summary

The HR practices under PMS are summarised in Table 32. As we saw at the start of this chapter, PMS is, in full, about intent, deployment, regulation, accountability and success.

As with other HR pillars, the processes and practices at ML1 are ad hoc. At ML1a, the fluid nature of practices suits the exploratory nature of the business and its actions. Performance is achieved through enthusiasm and the hands-on role of the founder. Behaviour is aligned by direct supervision, guidance and peer pressure. Employees are expected to get 'stuck in', enthusiastically. However, employees are only truly accountable for their immediate actions. As the organisation phases to ML2b, the dynamic nature of the business turns into ambiguity, if not chaos. Employees are expected to 'just do it'.

The functional structure and the narrow job design characteristic of ML2 help restore some semblance of order. The PMS at this level then reflects job and structural designs. Appraisals and SMART goals fit comfortably here, but as a 'bolt-on' system. The degree to which staff have 'done their duties' is captured in this documentation.

PMS moves centre stage at ML3. The plethora of KPIs and the strong sense of *individual* accountability supports the theme of continuous improvement. Employee success arises from delivering the numbers.

Finally, at ML4, the strategic balanced scorecard, the strategic competencies and the 360-degree approach renders the PMS holistic. Control is now more normative than metrical. Employees are accountable for becoming increasingly strategically competent – that is, being good organisational citizens.

Table 32. Summary – Performance Management Systems			
ML	*OML*	*HRML*	
1	Entrepreneurial Management	Initial	a) 'Make and sell' 　　Market survival and growth 　　Delivering immediate outputs 　　Informal real-time observational 　　feedback b) AOP 　　Budgetary delivery: revenue and cost 　　Basic accountancy controls 　　Ad hoc reporting on other issues 　　Increasingly fragmented PMS 　　Negative feedback only 　　No goal setting: 'just do it' 　　No codes of conduct 　　Correction for compliance errors 　　'Tolerance' of poor performance 　　Dismissal as prime 　　corrective tool
2	Process Management	Foundational	'Boundary controls': codes of conduct and MSOP 'MbO cascade' for managers SMART goals Appraisal as an annual bolt-on

			MYR FYR Combined PADR as 'duties done' Project management Project tracking (OTIF) SIP for sales staff linked to SIB PIP Disciplinary procedure
3	Proficiency Management	HR Agenda	Functional KPIs (input, process and output) Short-interval metrics CI targets and plans Operational BSC Visual management 'CRAGS' Closed-loop performance cycle: VTT-RCA-CAP-MoE IAR and ICR as 'delivering the numbers' Monthly 1-2-1 meetings PADR deconstructed Stretch goals 'CRAGS' PIP 'Expectations management' and 'management by consequence' 'Performance counts' The 5 Rs of 'management by consequences' Programme management Programme tracking by PMO Project benefits tracking
4	Systematic Management	Integrated People Strategy	Integrated EPM OSM Portfolio management Strategic BSC SKPIs cascaded 360-degree expectation approach Annual contribution conversation calendar Learning goals Appraisal as 'being and becoming' Normative controls

CHAPTER 7

EMPLOYEE ENGAGEMENT

Introduction

When discussing the HR strategic framework, we defined the two sides of EE as:

- Generating 'share of mind' for business messages,
- Securing employee commitment and
- Handling differences and conflict

- Building employee voice and participation and
- Building employee involvement and inclusion

In this chapter, we will discover how the firm attempts to gain the commitment of its employees to the enterprise's plans by using a range of HR practices that match the OML. The reader will be able to judge how the level of commitment is both enabled and constrained by all practices at each ML.

ML1 – Initial

At ML1a, engagement is direct between the founder and the relatively small number of employees at this level. Engagement will be strongly influenced by the founder's style, hence her employment model (see Table 3). Business messages are straight from the founder and tend to be delivered face-to-face. There is little need for any other more sophisticated channels. However, direct contact is a highly rich channel. Richness is defined as the capacity of a communications medium to change understanding.

The need to launch and survive is abundantly clear to all. Participation is by direct two-way interaction with the founder. As there is little specialisation at this level, everyone gets involved in virtually everything, so job enrichment is high – although, as a consequence, role ambiguity is also high. Any employee relations' issues are dealt with directly and immediately, even if there is a recognised trade union. Diversity and inclusion are, however, not on the agenda unless this is part and parcel of the founder's mission. The degree of individual involvement is determined by the founder's employment model. Broadly speaking, the commitment of employees to the enterprise is via the 'attachment' dimension of the founder's implicit blueprint (see Table 3).

As the firm moves into the emergent phase (ML1b), business messages are rapidly reduced to little more than verbal work instructions or directives as and when required. There is no consistency of messages at this level. As there is no plan as such, there is no source of consistent messages.

The direct contact that was characteristic of ML1a disappears. The lack of any new channels means that communications almost vanishes from the firm. Management and employees drift apart and the vacuum is filled by rumour and the grapevine.

Employee voice that was informal yet apparent at ML1a is lost at ML1b. There is virtually no voice for employees unless there is a recognised trade union, and here it is still minimal. Any voice granted by the organisation will merely be for compliance purposes: either external compliance with statutory consultation requirements or internal compliance to union agreements and demands. The employee relations (ER) climate is therefore likely to resemble the continuous ER conflict pattern. Disputes and grievances arise frequently due to the uncertainty, insecurity and inequity characteristic of this maturity level.

The employee involvement that was typical of ML1a fragments at ML1b. As job design becomes idiosyncratic and arbitrary, so job enlargement and enrichment are curtailed. Some jobs may retain the opportunity for a high level of job crafting. However, this is not the design or intent of the organisation. It is a legacy left over from the fluid nature of ML1a. Jobs gradually become circumscribed, but in a haphazard manner. This adds to the feeling of inequity at this maturity level.

At ML1b, diversity and inclusion is, at best, a compliance issue. The lack of systematic and disciplined practices leaves the company exposed to potentially discriminatory failings. The lack of any legal action is taken as a sign of legal and moral compliance, despite the underlying failings.

Overall, at ML1b, employees feel that they are kept in the dark. This 'mushroom' approach reduces employee commitment to the company to the bare minimum. They simply get on with it and get away with what they can.

ML2 – Foundational

As with all other aspects of HR practice at this maturity level, EE takes on a disciplined approach all of its own. Thus, at ML2, EE works by procedure. The overriding EE theme at ML2 is 'tell and sell'. The business puts in place a number of channels to correct the tendency for management and employees to drift apart, which became starkly apparent at ML1b.

As we saw in chapter three, there is no business plan as such. The plans are implicit in the organisation structure, job design, SOP and work schedules. These provide the prime communication content and principal channels. The only other source of news is from external shock. The enterprise's prime focus is on efficiency. In essence, it aims to establish a robust steady state with minimal novelty. Consequently, there is little in the way of 'news'. Hence, communications at ML2 consists of periods of the mundane punctuated by occasional dramas. In fact, some of the communication style and content at this level can border on the theatrical.

Work instructions support the process discipline of ML2. In some cases, these involve direct contact between employee and supervisor. However, in most modern contexts, such instructions come via a works management or enterprise resource planning (ERP) system. Direct instructions tend to be confrontational, whereas the anonymity of an ERP system takes the heat out of work instructions.

Business messages are by 'push' or 'send' channels. There is also a distinction between 'big' corporate messages and 'local' messages.

Local, 'small' messages deal with the routine, 'mundane' news. Hence, the ERP sends news of the work schedule; the SOP conveys the work process and tasks. Basic channels convey other routine messages or act as secondary back-up channels for other 'big' messages. The newsletter (hard copy or soft) and the noticeboard remain the backbone of regular organisational communications at this maturity level.

'Big' messages are transmitted occasionally across the whole firm. These convey business news. At ML2a, the emphasis is on local messages with the occasional business broadcast. So 'big' business messages tend not to align fully with local 'small' messages. At ML2b, with the adoption of common practices across the whole organisation, this misalignment dissipates to some extent.

'Big' messages announce key changes, e.g. in structure or senior appointments. Channels used include videos, conferences etc. In some cases, an element of drama is injected into the style of events, especially, as is often the case at this ML, if there is little in the way of fresh news to convey.

As we will discuss in the next section, the organisational structure at ML2 does not readily facilitate a cascade communication process. The many layers in the hierarchy naturally 'filter out' messages. So, senior management 'bypass' the structure in order to get their 'big' messages across. Three classic channels are often used: the roadshow (sometimes called town hall meetings), Direct Talk and the conference.

The CEO tours the organisation, perhaps annually, with an update on the business – a 'state of the nation' message to all employees in groups of 20–100, depending upon the availability of suitable venues. In each town hall, there is a limited amount of time for questions. As trust is not sufficiently developed at ML2, employees feel reluctant to raise issues in such an open forum.

In Direct Talk, a Director or VP has a round table meeting with 8–12 randomly chosen employees to brief them in a more confidential manner on business issues. This still tends to be a 'tell and sell' session, with a limited amount of time for questions. The employees are chosen from the same level of the organisation, e.g. operators, as 'diagonal slice' meetings are still alien to the company at this ML.

The conference emerges at ML2. This is organised especially for sales staff and for the senior management cadre. A lot of effort goes into planning and executing such events, but they still remain relatively moderate at best in terms of media richness. They are still of a 'tell and sell' style.

Overall, however, the most productive communications channel at ML2 is the effective management meeting. We discussed this under OE in chapter four. If management cannot hold regular disciplined meetings as functional teams at all organisational levels, then ML2 cannot be maintained in *any* part of the HRMM. The basics of good meeting management are thus essential. This enhances management efficiency and provides some material to communicate through the channels for each function. These messages also tend to be 'tell and sell' in nature.

Employee voice is limited at ML2. Basic procedures, such as the grievance procedure, are put in place to ensure that if an employee has a complaint there is a route whereby he can seek redress. Procedural justice is therefore seen to be done. In addition, the consultation procedure exists to enable collective issues of mutual concern to be discussed between management and worker representatives. This forum also provides a vehicle for change management (see chapter four).

Where there is trade union recognition, the grievance and consultation procedures may be partially or wholly covered in the union agreements. Where collective bargaining occurs, this will be on the basis of the traditional formal ER bargaining pattern concentrating on 'pay and rations'. There is a formal, written procedural agreement to govern union rights and processes and management obligations. Union relationships and engagement will be very formal. However, the range of agenda items covered with unions at this ML tends to be narrow. In the absence of a trade union, the company may create a works council to deal with collective issues. This also has a limited agenda at this ML.

To minimise grievances and disengagement, hygiene factors are addressed at ML2. Basic health, safety and welfare issues are actively tackled. If these basic employee needs are not dealt with, higher maturity levels cannot be attained. Hence, employee assistance programmes (EAP) are also found at ML2 to support employees who may be facing excessive stress or hardship.

As we saw in chapter four, jobs are narrow in terms of design. Work practices are also highly circumscribed by SOPs. In addition, there are many levels of supervision at ML2. These three factors severely restrict direct employee involvement. Decisions are made *for* most employees with limited opportunity for their input.

As with most other HR practices at this maturity level, inclusion is covered by a policy, setting out the firm's principles on diversity. However, as there is little in the way of planning at ML2, there are no schemes to shift any imbalance in the workforce. Practices tend to concentrate on ensuring bias is eliminated from recruitment and other HR practices.

In reality, the firm at ML2 wants employees to 'commit' to the SOP and the work schedule. There is no grand plan by which to align employees' endeavours. Hence, employees cannot be expected to commit more than their conformance to the enterprise's systems.

ML3 – HR Agenda

There is a shift in the theme of EE from 'tell and sell' to 'listen' at ML3 and the richness of communication channels is enhanced. Messages remain mostly SBU and functional in nature, but with a strategic flavour that was absent at ML2.

The company has a richer source of information at this level to feed its communication channels. The SBU 'strategy', the array of KPIs, the CI agenda and the balanced scorecard (BSC) offer more sources of news. As we have seen, performance management is the dominant theme at ML3 (see chapter six). To match the performance cycle, an annual communication calendar is established that mirrors the timetable for the BSC. Communication is thus built into the fabric of the organisation. In fact, the timetable for the BSC acts as a discipline for *all* management activities. The calendar captures all the communication events, processes and activities for the full year.

The delayered structure we discussed in chapters three and four facilitates the cascading of messages at ML3. Firstly, the clearer definition of accountabilities by organisational level means that each level can add value to any cascaded business message. Secondly, the fewer layers that a message has to pass through, the greater the chances of that message getting to its target audience. As we discussed above, the organisational layers in ML2 mean that messages get 'filtered out', hence cascades do not work at ML2. Thirdly, the abundance of KPIs at ML3 offers material to create messages that fit the circumstances of each department and each level of employees. Fourthly, as we have mentioned, the discipline of the BSC provides the timetable and thus the stimulus to communicate. As with PMS, there is now a natural flow to communication activities.

The cascade process enables a monthly series of briefings. In some cases, these are built into existing management and team meetings. In other cases, new briefing sessions are scheduled (i.e. built into the roster) in line with the communications calendar. Such briefings have a permanent '4 Ps' agenda: performance, progress, policies and people. Performance is fed by the KPIs. Progress is fed by the continuous improvement (CI) agenda and the projects that are a key element of this maturity level.

At senior level, quarterly leadership briefings are held to update executives on strategies and to refocus efforts. The SBU and functional nature of the organisation can fragment energies and split loyalties. Hence, the senior players endeavour to build a more corporate spirit through these leadership briefings. However, these still only have moderate media richness.

Of a more productive nature, at the operational level, morning team meetings ensure that each shift is updated on the issues of the day. Problems are highlighted and work tasks reassigned to accommodate for such issues. This, however, remains a 'send' channel.

Voice channels are broadened at ML3. The works council develops beyond the basic procedural model at ML2. With medium-term SBU and functional strategies crafted and active, there is material to discuss and consult on. Employee participation extends to cover a wider range of agenda items, often beyond that which is required by statute. Management proactively consults on significant matters of mutual interest. Where there is trade union recognition, such consultation involves the union representatives. In such circumstances, there is extensive engagement with the unions, formally and informally. However, while the SBU endeavours to build productive relations with its works council, HQ can hijack the change agenda. With the alternating phases of decentralisation and centralisation (see chapter four), reorganisations are periodically imposed on the SBUs by HQ. This can have a damaging effect upon the relationships with the works council and with trade unions.

The firm introduces occasional listen channels. Management sponsors focus groups where they wish to tap into the opinions of employees on specific topics of concern. These are facilitated by independent third parties, rather than line managers, in order to create a safe environment for employees to express their views. This enables management to access qualitative data on specific issues.

To access quantitative data on EE, management sponsors employee surveys, typically on an annual basis. Such surveys are generic, so allowing the company to benchmark with industry norm groups. Generic surveys are also a logical choice at ML3 as the enterprise has yet to establish the strategic competencies that add value for the business. This is not attained until ML4 (see below). Issues and problems highlighted through the survey results lead to the commissioning of related projects. These are overseen by the PMO.

The Direct Talk channel at ML2 evolves into, what we call, a Director Forum channel. Here, a Director or VP chairs a roundtable discussion with a randomly selected group of 8–12 employees. However, unlike the Direct Talk channel (see above), this is a listening session. The Director facilitates the discussion rather than briefing the employees. There is a separate briefing channel, so the director forum is focused on tapping into the opinions and feelings of employees. This is a feedback channel. Agenda items may be topical and current – "What did you think of the CEO's video broadcast last month?" – or may be more general – "What's it like to work around here?".

HR also runs its own voice channel. So-called HR breakfast meetings enable HR to tap into 'field intelligence'. Again, a randomly selected group of 8–12 employees are invited to an informal meeting to raise issues and discuss topics of concern or interest. The discussion is entirely confidential. The intent is not to build up a 'shopping list' of employee grievances, but to assess the morale of employees and uncover generic issues.

In support of the CI agenda, characteristic of this maturity level, a suggestion scheme fits at ML3. This offers employees the opportunity to put forward ideas for improvement. The scheme feeds the programme boards that review projects. Quality circles are also adopted on an occasional basis to support the CI agenda. These also act as embryonic self-managed teams that come to full fruition at ML4 (see chapter two). The suggestion scheme also aligns with the recognition scheme introduced at this ML (see chapter nine).

The narrow jobs of ML2 are moderately broadened roles at ML3, horizontally and, more important, vertically (see chapter four). Thus, employees become more involved in local issues that directly affect them through job enlargement.

The weight of KPIs helps shift the diversity agenda at ML3. SBUs and functions now have medium-term plans, including workforce plans. This enables a more proactive approach to inclusion. The external benchmarking allows the firm to measure any imbalances across its own employee groups. Corrective action is now actively pursued.

The SBUs and their functions have clear strategies and targets at ML3. The whole life cycle of the enterprise is based upon continuous improvement. The EE agenda at this maturity level attempts to engender the instrumental commitment of employees towards this performance ethos.

ML4 – Integrated People Strategy

At ML4, EE matures into a full 'engage' mode. 'Dialogue' is the ruling theme. Employees benefit from more direct involvement. Management adopts communication channels of greater media richness, many driven by employees themselves.

The integrated enterprise strategy provides ample material to share with employees. This enables a shift towards a clearly articulated employer brand and towards the internal marketing of the strategy and the brand. The brand now feeds channels not normally classified (at lower maturity levels) as 'communications', e.g. recruitment, induction, training, rewards etc. The use of multiple channels improves the richness of both the media selected and the message. Examples of communication channels are set out in Table 33.

Table 33. Communication Channel Richness	
High	Face-to-face 1-2-1 meetings Workshops Seminars Director Forums Focus Groups
Medium	Team briefings Personalised statements Helplines Guidance literature Conferences Online literature
Low	Emails Surveys Videos Newsletters Direct mail Posters Noticeboards

The annual communications calendar is now at the enterprise level rather than at the SBU level, as it was at ML3. This calendar integrates all activities, not just core communications. Thus, what started as a local discipline at ML2 with the effective monthly management meeting is now a comprehensive integrated discipline across the entire organisation.

The creation of the vision and values, and of the strategic competency framework now informs the employee survey. While some of the generic questions used at ML3 may be retained for benchmarking purposes, the business is now able to tailor the survey to the competencies it has identified as adding value to the firm. Fewer questions are required, allowing the enterprise to conduct pulse surveys on a more frequent basis than, say, once a year. This enables the company to tap into the views and sentiments of employees more readily.

The relationship with recognised trade unions advances to a full partnership model. If there is a works council, the relationship is similar. Consultation takes place on a wide range of issues and especially on any statements of future intent (see chapter four). Strategic, long-term issues are dealt with. A sample range of agenda items is set out in Table 34.

Table 34. Employee Voice Generic Agenda Items
The economic and financial situation
Employment patterns and workforce levels
Collective redundancies
New working methods and productivity initiatives
Health, safety and welfare arrangements
Training
Transfers of undertakings
Grading and job evaluation
Rates of pay
Terms & conditions
Promotional and transfer arrangements
Procedural arrangements
Working hours, holidays and rosters
Overtime working and arrangements
Work allocation
Job design

The creation of temporary and permanent self-managed teams (SMT), which we discussed in chapters two and four, enables employees to be even more directly involved in their work through job enrichment. Decisions that have a direct impact on the employee are delegated to the lowest possible level. So, holidays, work assignments, work rotation, training etc. are decided within the SMT. In fact, the high degree of autonomy enables employees to become architects of communications themselves. Communities of practice (CoP) arise, facilitated by internal social media. The lattice structure of the organisation demands that employees are able to connect with others who can support and assist in the execution of work. Reliance on purely formal channels would atrophy corporate performance. Employees are thus able to crowdsolve.

The strategic planning characteristic of ML4 feeds the inclusion agenda. This broader and more long-term perspective enables positive action plans, which ensure the business becomes more representative of its diverse external communities.

As we indicated in chapters three and five, the prime focus at ML4 is on the vision and values. Employees are selected for their fit with the culture. They are developed in line with the strategic competencies. The commitment the firm seeks at this level is the personal identification with, and internalisation of, those competencies and values. The quid pro quo of this level of commitment is that employees have a 'right to know' as full organisational partners.

Summary

The EE practices at each maturity level are set out in Table 35. Throughout this chapter, we have seen that EE consists of business messages and channels, employee participation and voice, the employee relations climate, employee involvement and inclusion, and the commensurate level of employee commitment.

At ML1a, EE practices centre upon the founder. Her style seals the overall engagement approach. At ML1b, engagement is ad hoc, fragmented and compliance-oriented. Commitment is minimal.

At ML2, the theme shifts to a 'tell and sell' model. There is an emphasis on the 'big' business message and the local 'small' message. This is very much a 'push' approach. Local communications rely heavily on the effective management meeting. As with all HR pillars, procedures figure greatly at ML2. Commitment is focused on conformance to the SOP and work schedule.

At ML3, the SBU strategies provide a more ready source for business messages. The delayered organisational structure enables the effective and meaningful cascade of messages. Employee participation becomes more active in comparison to the passive approach at ML2, hence the theme of 'listen'. Commitment is instrumental.

Finally, at ML4, the integrated enterprise strategy and associated values facilitates more meaningful communications, participation and involvement. The SMT, employer branding and the high degree of delegation support the theme of 'dialogue'. Commitment is through identification and internalisation.

Table 35. Summary – Employee Engagement			
ML	*OML*	*HRML*	
1	Entrepreneurial Management	Initial	a) Direct message from the founder High informal job enrichment and involvement Informal team engagement Informal face-to-face dialogue and voice High media richness b) Verbal work instructions and directives Ambiguous business messages Limited, ad hoc or no 'voice' Statutory information & consultation compliance only TU negotiations, if forced Continuous ER conflict pattern Low worker involvement Disputes and grievances due to uncertainty, insecurity and inequity Diversity compliance only Minimal commitment
2	Process Management	Foundational	'Tell & sell' theme a) 'Big' corporate messages and 'small' local messages misalign b) Alignment of local and corporate messages Limited news Routine messages Dramatic communications 'Push' business messages Basic channels: newsletters and noticeboards Low media richness Effective management meetings Work instructions via ERP system Deep hierarchy 'filters out' cascade messages Roadshows, town halls, events, videos Conferences: management and sales Minimal voice channels

			Direct talk Health, safety and welfare hygiene factors addressed EAP Grievance procedure Consultation procedure Procedural justice Works council constitution and/or formal TU recognition Traditional formal TU bargaining pattern: 'pay and rations' Conformance commitment
3	Proficiency Management	HR Agenda	'Listen' theme SBU agenda messages Annual SBU communications calendar Cascade messages Monthly team briefings 4 Ps briefing agenda HR 'breakfast' meetings Quarterly leadership briefings Operational daily/shift meetings Works council: wider agenda Extensive TU engagement Focus groups Generic employee survey Director forums Suggestion schemes Quality circles Formal job enlargement Formal diversity plans Instrumental commitment
4	Systematic Management	Integrated People Strategy	'Dialogue' theme Strategic business messages Employer brand Employee value proposition Internal marketing Integrated annual calendar: meetings, BSC, communications etc. Strategic bespoke employee survey Pulse surveys TU partnership model/Works Council Procedural and substantive justice Job enrichment Direct involvement in decisions affecting employees

			Communities of practice Crowdsolving 'Right to know' Commitment through identification and internalisation

CHAPTER 8

EMPLOYEE DEVELOPMENT

Introduction

We have described the purpose of ED as:

- Raising people capability in terms of knowledge, skills and process abilities
- Establishing personal competence,
- Developing performance excellence and
- Progressing the employee development journey

In this chapter, we will explain the extent to which the business supports the personal development of its employees in terms of knowledge, skills and process abilities. Current capability represents future potential performance – hence, the firm may invest in its people where it sees the need for enhanced performance. We will see the degree to which the enterprise actually invests in its people and how this changes as we move through the maturity levels.

ML1 – Initial

In the start-up phase, employees are hired for the critical skills and aptitudes they already possess and that the firm requires immediately. As the business searches for the right way to do things, learning is through informal on-the-job training (OJT) and by trial and error. Learning is highly experiential, but ad hoc.

As the business transitions to the emergent phase (ML1b), employee development remains ad hoc. Learning for new hires is by 'sitting next to Nellie' – that is, by simple observation of an experienced operator. Hence the acquired skills etc. are entirely dependent upon the quality of that operator. Bad practices can thus persist for generations. As there are no SOPs at this maturity level, inconsistencies and variability are perpetuated by this approach to learning. Conversely, where there is no experienced operator to learn from, development is through the 'university of hard knocks' as individuals are just 'dropped in the deep end'. This is development by the 'sink or swim' methodology.

There is limited support from the organisation, except where compliance training is required by external parties or by statute. ED remains spasmodic or absent. Any ED activity will depend upon the bias or penchant of the CEO. So, sudden initiatives may apparently necessitate some ED intervention, usually sourced externally, with little training needs analysis (TNA) or rationale. The initiative fades away, perhaps to be replaced by another, possibly again supported by some learning intervention.

Contrastingly, development may be lavished upon the favoured few. Junior apprentice 'heroes' may be fed excessive development support while most are starved of such help.

ML2 – Foundational

To complement other pillars in the HRMM at this maturity level, there are two themes that drive ED interventions: 'establishing operational effectiveness' and 'developing managerial skills'.

The process discipline and the proliferation of SOPs both demand consistent and repeatable tasks, and standardisation of skills. The narrow job design reduces most jobs to a small set of routine duties. This all lends itself to basic job training (BJT) modules for the majority of employees. The aim is to produce personal competency within weeks, if not days, of a new hire starting.

BJT is reinforced back on the shop floor by first line managers' OJT. This is one of the basic tasks of first line managers or assistants specifically assigned this role. Hence, managers and assistants are also trained on the basic tasks of their subordinates. Periodically, OJT acts as refresher training for operators to ensure continued conformance to the SOPs.

Hence, the second theme driving learning interventions at ML2 is 'developing management skills'. As we have just seen, first line managers carry out OJT as a form of basic *task* coaching. This is part of the core curriculum for managers. At ML2, the curriculum is based upon the requirements of the first line manager. It is assumed that this is suitable for all managers regardless of hierarchical level. This core curriculum is designed to build personal competency in the core responsibilities for all managers (see Table 11). The outline of a typical core management curriculum is set out in Table 36. This curriculum will be reinforced in policies and procedural guidelines, and also in a basic manager's handbook. This core curriculum acts as a foundation for higher maturity levels. The exact content varies in sophistication between the different maturity levels. Also, as with other practices, the content differs across units at ML2a, but is common across the whole organisation at ML2b.

ED activities also support induction. This provides new hires with the basic general knowledge about the company. Where an employee transfers from one department to another, an internal mini-induction session is held to ensure specific information is imparted and the employee is integrated into her new section.

All ED interventions are informed by objective training needs analysis (TNA). This ensures the optimal use of training resources and the most appropriate learning intervention is designed.

All formal training is logged on the employee's record. Training required for compliance and statutory purposes is timetabled to ensure that re-accreditation takes place prior to any legally set deadline.

At ML2, an employee is either a trainee or a qualified operator. Training and work are separate. Once qualified, there is little development on offer other than OJT.

ML3 – HR Agenda

ED at ML3 is driven by the additional themes of 'enhancing leadership', 'CI support' and 'performance enhancement'.

The delayering of the organisational structure into the (maximum of) seven levels of role responsibility (see Table 4) allows a more sophisticated approach to management training. The core curriculum we discussed under ML2 is now adapted to take into account the different responsibilities at the different managerial levels, hence the additional theme of 'enhancing leadership' that drives ED at this ML.

The career ladders that we discussed under calibre and talent (see chapter five) also offer a more robust framework for ED interventions. The competencies help define the leadership qualities desired at the different organisational levels. This further informs the design of ED interventions.

Table 36. Core Management Curriculum			
Responsibility	*Component*	*Knowledge*	*Skills*
Securing resources	Budget setting and control	Budgetary process Financial regulations and procedures Accountancy calendar	Negotiating Monitoring Numeracy
	Equipment	Work processes SSW	
Measurement and reporting system		Measurement systems Report types	Monitoring Feedback
Staffing		Contracts of employment Terms & conditions Employment law	
	Resourcing	Budgeted headcount Job description Person specification Recruitment policy Employment law	Interviewing techniques
	Attendance management	T&A System Attendance policy & procedure RTW procedure Shifts and holiday rosters Rehabilitation procedure Occupational health services	Absence analysis RTW interviewing
Performance management	Workload allocation	Planning systems Work systems SOPs SSW Work assignments Projects	Task allocation and rostering Work instructions Basic project management
	Tracking	PADR process Performance management policy	Monitoring Appraising
	Feedback		Observation Measurement and assessment Dialogue constructive feedback

	Corrective action	PIP Discipline procedure	Investigating Counselling Disciplining
Employee development		SOPs Person specification Learning interventions L&D curricula	Basic coaching
	Sourcing training	PADR process Training solutions catalogue	Competency rating Basic TNA
	Coaching		Basic task coaching
Employee communications	Briefing		Preparing a brief Giving a speech Handling questions
	Presentation		Presenting
	Meeting management	PACER	Chairing
Employee relations		Discrimination laws	
	Management by walking about (MBWA)		Listening Influencing skills
	Grievances	Grievance procedure	Investigating Conducting a grievance meeting
Reward & recognition	Rewards	Reward policies Authority levels	
	Recognition		Feedback
	Payroll rules	Payroll deadlines Contract of employment Terms & conditions Payroll exception reporting Expenses	
Problem-solving		Problem-solving techniques	Analysis Decision-making

Peer relations			Collaborating
External liaison		Stakeholders	Collaborating
Change management		Planned change models Consultation procedure Contracts of Employment Terms & Conditions	Consulting Handling objections

There is also a focus on the top leadership group and HIPOs identified under the calibre agenda at this ML. The leadership group is approximately the top 1 per cent of the internal population. Each senior player has a leadership development plan (LDP) to identify strengths and development needs, and to craft bespoke solutions to meet their learning objectives.

HIPOs were simply identified at ML2. At ML3, they are developed. Thus, HIPOs have individual development plans (IDP). Such IDPs offer a wide range of options. These will be bespoke solutions tailored for each individual's needs (see chapter five for calibre actions).

When discussing performance management systems in chapter six, we saw that the IAR and ICR are focused on performance alone. The combined PADR at ML2 causes development goals to be crowded out by the other performance-oriented SMART goals. Thus, personal development plan (PDP) emerges at ML3 in a basic form. This is primarily focused on developing the functionally oriented competencies that we discussed under calibre and talent (see chapter five). The competencies are those that relate to the employee's current level of role responsibility (I-VII). Learning interventions are crafted to help employees develop their competency and thus their performance in their current role. This suite of interventions brings the theme of 'performance excellence' alive, i.e. PET. Line managers play a part in this as they deliver on-the-job *performance* coaching. An annual discussion between employee and manager helps craft the full PDP. The PDP then feeds the annual development plans of each function and SBU.

ED at ML3 is also driven by the theme of 'CI alignment'. Continuous improvement requires ED support on a number of fronts. Firstly, managers and employees need training on the array of tools used to identify opportunities and solutions for CI, e.g. Six Sigma, Lean manufacturing, Triz, TQM, Taguchi methods, programme management etc. Secondly, ED helps build the CI toolbox needed to support each specific programme and the related projects. Thirdly, as business processes are re-engineered, BJT needs to be redesigned to reflect the new methods of working so that new hires and existing employees are qualified to operate the new SOP.

In support of the desire to benchmark with 'best in class', managers and technical staff participate in external study tours and visits to glean new and innovative practices that can be adapted to and by the business.

ML4 – Integrated People Strategy

The organisation at this maturity level is driven by the theme of 'supporting personal development'. The ED activities found at ML4 will resemble those of a learning organisation where knowledge management is actively pursued. The organisation seeks proactively to capture and utilise the intellectual property held by its human capital.

1-2-1 meetings in the business are now strongly developmental in nature. We partially covered this in chapter seven when we discussed the annual conversation calendar at ML4. The resultant PDP focuses on developing each employee's strategic competencies. As a learning organisation, there is no separation of performance and learning as there was at ML2. In fact, most development is seen as on-the-job, following the 70:20:10 rule. That is, 70 per cent of learning is on-the-job, 20 per cent comes from peers and mentors, and only 10 per cent is from formal learning, classroom or online. The mix of learning interventions reflects this rule. Much of the learning thus becomes self-directed and blended. Also, career development experiences (CDE) are identified and created to enable personal development following the 70:20:10 rule. Managers at this ML contribute to personal development through *competency* coaching.

Career development training (CDT) is also crafted to support the employee through the full employee development life cycle or employee journey.

All the different training categories that have been created at this maturity level and below now come together in a comprehensive format – an 'A, B, C, D' of employee development (see Table 37). This covers the four categories of development interventions that have been built up through the four maturity levels and the specific requirements at each organisational accountability level – one to seven. Hence, an organisational employee development matrix can be crafted. An example framework for this is set out in Table 38.

Table 37. Categories of Development Interventions		
Code	*Type*	*Definition*
A	BJT	Learning interventions that equip the individual with the knowledge, skills and process abilities to manage the first 100 days in a new role and to meet the minimum standards of performance (MSOP) for the role
A+	BJT+	Learning interventions that build the knowledge, skills and process abilities essential to achieving personal competency in the core accountabilities of the role
B	OJT	Learning interventions that reinforce and update knowledge, skills and process abilities in order to maintain personal competency for an existing occupant of the role
C	PET	Learning interventions that build knowledge, skills and process abilities to establish mastery in the role Mastery is benchmarked as upper quartile performance in the role Full professional or equivalent status for the role or organisational level is achieved through this level of intervention
D	CDT	Learning interventions that prepare the individual for the transition to roles at the next organisational level or for a lateral move and to give her an insight into the demands and requirements of such a new role through developing the relevant competencies and learning agility

Table 38. Organisational Employee Development Matrix					
Type of development interventions	A	A+	B	C	D
	BJT	BJT+	OJT	PET	CDT
Organisational Level of Responsibility					
I					
II					
III					
IV					
V					
VI					
VII					

The creation of self-managed teams (SMT) at ML4 requires ED support. Problem-solving and project management become part of the SMT's duties. Multi-skilling is at the core of the formation of SMTs. All of this necessitates the crafting of ED interventions. Training itself may well be a skill that is embedded in the SMT. As we discussed in chapter six, the skills matrix supports the SMT. This is both a feature of ED and PMS at this ML.

Mentoring is systematically built into the portfolio of development solutions. Subject matter experts (SME) are identified and encouraged to act as formal mentors. They are trained to carry out this role.

Induction, which was introduced at ML2, now becomes orientation. New hires will have been recruited for their 'good fit' with the strategic competencies – the 'culture'. This is further inculcated through orientation soon after the new hire's engagement.

Summary

The HR practices associated with ED as summarised in Table 39.

In this chapter, we have seen how HR practices increase in sophistication across the maturity levels. At ML1, learning is experiential. Learning is by trial and error. We saw in chapter five, when discussing C&T, that the firm hires in the skills it needs. The lack of defined roles and business processes also means that there is little point in devising formal development interventions.

At ML2, the enterprise is focused on operational efficiency and stability. The range of SOPs and the well defined, if narrow, jobs lend themselves to basic development interventions. This is driven by the theme of 'establishing operational effectiveness'. The equivalent theme driving management training is 'developing managerial skills', but focused especially at the level of first line management.

The focus shifts at ML3. 'Continuous improvement' is the order of the day and ED is realigned to this theme. SOPs are regularly updated, so development interventions follow suit.

At ML4, the theme changes to 'supporting personal development', in order to grow the strategic competencies and progress the employee through her development journey.

ML	OML	HRML	
**Table 39. Summary – Employee Development**			
1	Entrepreneurial Management	Initial	a) Learning by trial and error Experiential learning Informal OJT b) Ad hoc, spasmodic or no training Sitting next to Nellie Sink or swim approach Compliance training Personal development for the few favoured 'heroes'
2	Process Management	Foundational	'Establishing operational effectiveness' 'Developing managerial skills' BJT: SOP training for core operational processes OJT for reinforcement Task coaching Core curriculum for (first line) managers Induction TNA Training records Project management training Managers' handbook
3	Proficiency Management	HR Agenda	'Enhancing leadership' 'CI support' 'Performance enhancement' LDP for senior managers IDP for HIPOs Basic PDP separated out from PADR Performance coaching CI toolbox training BJT competency-based training BJT updated for SOP modified by CI projects PET Core curriculum for each hierarchical level Programme management training External study tours

4	Systematic Management	Integrated People Strategy	'Supporting personal development' Knowledge management Learning organisation Developmental 1-2-1 meetings 70:20:10 rule CDE CDT Organisational ED Matrix Self-directed learning Blended learning Multi-skilling and project management training for SMT Skills matrix Mentoring Portfolio management training Competency coaching Orientation

CHAPTER 9

REWARD & RECOGNITION

Introduction

We have defined the two sides of R&R as:

- Building competitiveness in the chosen employment market(s),
- Delivering the employment deal(s) and
- Creating vehicles for 'motivational messages'

- Maintaining a 'good' standard of living and
- Attaining 'due' recognition and 'just' deserts

As can be seen, the definition of R&R includes the full range of 'motivations'. We will, however, divide the discussion into two. Firstly, in this chapter, we will cover the topics traditionally associated with compensation & benefits. Secondly, we will cover the full range of motivations in the next chapter. Our reasoning is quite simple. Motivations cover *all* HR pillars and are enabled by all HR pillars. Therefore, motivations warrant discussion in a separate chapter. Further, as we will see, managing the total 'motivation agenda' only becomes fully and explicitly open to the organisation at ML4. In this chapter, we will describe how reward practices grow in sophistication as we move through the maturity levels. We will also see how the focus changes.

R&R is a very broad field. So, the discussion will be confined to the salient differences in R&R practices that distinguish the four maturity levels. We will thus omit some of the more esoteric aspects of R&R. Hence, we will cover salary determination and progression, contingent pay, some non-financial rewards and recognition.

ML1 – Initial

At start-up (ML1a), the rewards are relatively basic. Salary is virtually the only feature for the vast majority of employees. The firm does not have the infrastructure to manage much else. The salary offered to new starters will be whatever is expedient at the time. Thus, 'benchmarking' is whatever pay secures the new hire *and* what the firm can afford at that time.

Benefits are limited, being statutory only or absent. The business carries out basic payroll administration if for no other reason than to deduct tax and manage its own cash – that is, to comply with external and internal regulations. The foundational HR processes at this level are, firstly, from hours worked to gross pay and, secondly, from gross pay to net pay. Depending upon the blueprint of the founder (see Table 3), some start-ups grant an equity stake to the founding team.

As the organisation phases into ML1b, there is still no coherent reward structure. Securing staff for a small business is challenging, so expediency results in wide variations in offers and reward packages. Further, if the business acquires other firms, the inherited reward structure is usually left intact. Hence, an accumulation of past practices leads to a fragmented reward structure with no guiding principles. This leads to a strong sense of inequity, feelings of relative deprivation and resentment. Formal and informal grievances arise because individuals doing roughly the same job are rewarded differently. There is no rhyme or reason to explain the current reward set-up or the differences in individual packages. To compound this, management see money as the solution to all problems. To hold onto staff who threaten to leave, management throw money at the problem. This only exacerbates the underlying issue of inequity.

Bonuses and other rewards tend to be invested in heroes and their heroic efforts (see chapter three). Thus, the implication is that action heroes are prized and encouraged. As we have discussed already, this behaviour on the part of management reinforces the prevailing leadership model at this ML (see chapter five).

Payroll administration remains the only coherent R&R system at ML2b. However, as we have discussed, this is nothing to do with motivation and all to do with financial controls and compliance.

ML2 – Foundational

As we have indicated, in all other pillars of the HRMM at ML2a, a local functional approach is followed. However, R&R is different (Curtis et al, p.32). The chronic reward problems that build up at ML1 must be resolved otherwise all other HR practices would be contaminated by the heightened sense of inequity. Hence, the organisation implements a unified company-wide reward structure. A sense of parity across the whole organisation is established and maintained. This enables all other practices at ML2 to be implemented and, ultimately, for higher ML to be attainable. However, this unified reward structure does not constitute a 'reward strategy'. The only guiding principle is conformity to a common corporate template. There is, as such, no explicit or underlying psychological contract, employer brand, employee value proposition etc.

Clearly, depending on the extent of the problems created at ML1b, the reform of the reward structure can take years. Employees usually regard any isolated proposal to change rewards to be highly suspect. This whole process needs careful communication and change management, and is usually best linked to other broader changes in the enterprise such as restructures etc.

As mentioned above, the aim of a unified reward structure is to create parity, both horizontal and vertical. Horizontally, all jobs of a similar 'size' are placed on the same reward packages. Vertically, jobs of a larger 'size' are put onto packages that are proportionately larger. All of this is achieved using a number of HR reward practices.

Firstly, the functional structure lends itself to establishing job families. Secondly, a process of job evaluation achieves 'job sizing'. Thirdly, given the profile of the job sizing exercise, a grading structure is adopted. Fourthly, grades are benchmarked with the chosen labour market to assess competitiveness. A single market is chosen as this helps establish internal parity. For example, a breakfast cereal business may choose to benchmark with the national food manufacturing labour market. Fifthly, the enterprise chooses a pay policy position, e.g. upper quartile in the civil engineering labour market. Sixthly, partially derived from the benchmarking, a terms & conditions (T&C) matrix is explicitly or implicitly established. This matrix sets out the spot salary or salary bands that will apply at each grade and the range of benefits that will apply at each grade. It is not unusual to have different benefits apply at higher grades: e.g. share options at executive level, but no overtime entitlement; bonus schemes at managerial grades, but not at operator level. A sample T&C matrix is set out in Table 40.

As can be seen, the salary bands tend to be relatively narrow at ML2. For some grades, the rate may be fixed at a spot salary. This is because, at ML2, there is little to differentiate employees in the same grade except by length of service.

G	Min	Max	O	B	L	P	D	R	C
16	19,238	21,161	Y	n/a	N	Self	x 2	Std.	n/a
17	20,777	22,854	Y	n/a	N	Self	x 2	Std.	n/a
18	22,590	24,849	Y	n/a	N	Self	x 2	Std.	n/a
19	25,907	28,497	Y	n/a	N	Self	x 2	Std.	n/a
20	28,985	31,883	N	n/a	N	Self	x 2	Std.	n/a
21	34,673	38,140	N	10%	N	Family	x 3	Std.	n/a
22	39,848	43,832	N	10%	N	Family	x 3	Std.	n/a
23	45,315	49,846	N	20%	N	Family	x 3	Std.	A
24	54,338	59,771	N	20%	N	Family	x 3	Std.	A
25	64,688	71,156	N	30%	N	Family	x 3	Std.	B
26	77,625	85,388	N	40%	Y	Family	x 4	Exec.	C
27	89,010	97,911	N	40%	Y	Family	x 4	Exec.	C
28	104,535	114,989	N	50%	Y	Family	x 4	Exec.	D
29	122,488	134,737	N	50%	Y	Family	x 4	Exec.	D
30	143,195	157,514	N	75%	Y	Family	x 4	Exec.	E

Table 40. Terms & Conditions Matrix

KEY

G = Grade

Min = Minimum in salary range (£)

Max = Maximum in salary range (£)

O = Overtime eligibility

B = On-target bonus as percentage of salary

L = Long-term incentive entitlement

P = Private medical insurance cover

D = Death in service as multiple of salary

R = Retirement pension entitlement

C = Car list entitlement

So, at ML2, the reward structure becomes highly standardised and bureaucratic in feel. The desire not to repeat the errors of ML1b, with its chaotic inequitable reward practices, means that the business keeps a tight rein on reward activities. Thus, authority to change rewards is reserved to fairly senior executives, high up in the organisation. Multiple signatures are required and there is no discretion for local managers to change rewards. To manage this, a payroll change form (PCF) is created at this ML. Any request to change an employee's payroll status requires this supporting documentation in order to seek senior authorisation. Clearly, this limits local managers' ability to reward individual contribution. Further, the lack of short-interval *individual* performance management at ML2 makes senior management even more reluctant to grant power in this regard to lower levels of management. If there is no way to distinguish *individual* contribution or worth, then there is no objective basis to differentiate *individual* rewards. Clearly, this is in stark contrast to the level of discretion at local level for other practices, especially at ML2a. This creates tension within the managerial hierarchy.

Reward is regarded as an annual event. Pay rises tend to reflect the year-on-year change in the cost of living, all other things being equal. There is virtually no deviation from this blanket approach. Management reserves the right to withhold an individual's pay rise if his performance is unsatisfactory or to award a higher rise where performance is outstanding. However, these powers are hardly ever used. This is partially due to the difficulty in measuring individual performance and partially to avoid the sense of inequity characteristic of ML1b.

Contingent pay comes in three forms: short-term incentive payment (STIP), sales incentive bonus (SIB) and overtime.

STIP is payable to senior managers and executives. While it is often referred to as an incentive payment, it is not linked to individual performance at all at ML2. It is, in essence, an at-risk, profit-related annual payment. Generally the link is to the profits of the overall enterprise, as at ML2 it is impractical to measure the contribution of any one functional unit to the profit line. The actual financial metric used may vary from year to year depending upon the requirements or whims of the business. This persistent reforming of the STIP scheme occurs in an attempt to better motivate managers to hit the profit target. However, the word 'incentive' is misplaced at ML2 as few managers can genuinely affect the top-level performance metrics and individual effort does not translate into actual results. The formula for payment varies across schemes, but generally is a straight-line relationship between profit and percentage payout, with a threshold below which no payment is made and an upper cap that constrains the maximum payout. Payment is expressed as a percentage of base salary. Thus, STIP at this maturity level is a glorified profit-share scheme for managers. Again, the firm may reserve the right to withhold payment of STIP to an individual manager, but this is rarely done.

SIB, on the other hand, is a true incentive payment. We saw under performance management systems (see chapter six) that sales staff have a sales incentive plan (SIP). There is a hard-formula relationship between hitting financial targets, such as sales revenue, and SIB payments. Again, there is usually a lower threshold and an upper cap. Payment may be expressed in terms of a percentage of base salary or an actual cash amount for on-target performance. The payment curve may be a straight-line relationship, or may have accelerators or decelerators built into the curve. The sophistication of the design varies across organisations, but the underlying models are very similar. Payment is usually for the performance in the prior month. Most schemes 'bank' monthly payments for performance over the on-target level. If the 'bank' remains in credit, then this is paid after the end of the performance year. This 'banking' ensures that the sales person is not 'overpaid' in early months if she subsequently underperforms in later months. The employee's SIB for the full year will thus match the overall sales performance across the whole year.

Operational ('non-exempt') staff are usually entitled to overtime for hours worked beyond the standard working week. At ML2, this is usually the only variable pay for shop floor workers.

Recognition tends only to be for tenure at ML2. This may include a longer holiday entitlement for those over a given service threshold, e.g. five years' service and for every five years thereafter. Long service awards (LSA) may be via a cash award or gift and/or a certificate. A dinner at an award ceremony is not uncommon. Again, the inability of the firm to differentiate individual performance inhibits the creation of a more comprehensive, formal recognition scheme. Such a reward mechanism is misplaced at ML2.

A basic set of benefits may exist. Insurance-backed benefits, such as death in service, healthcare plans, sick pay, ill-health retirement plans and pension plans etc. commonly apply. These may differ across the grades. The company may not provide these benefits if there is adequate provision by the state government. Such benefits are set out in the T&C matrix (see Table 40). However, it is worth noting that this document is confined to HR departments at ML2. Transparency does not emerge until ML3 for reasons we will cover in the next section.

The reward package is captured in company publications. Rewards that are offered to most, if not all, employees, are set out in an employee handbook. Those that are available for only a few are set out in the contract of employment for these grades.

ML3 – HR Agenda

R&R takes on a more sophisticated appearance at this maturity level. It becomes a comprehensible and transparent reward structure. That is, all can openly access and understand the format and content. The reward manager under ML2 may feel reluctant to be so transparent about the reward structure at that level, as much of her work involves ironing out all of the inequities inherited from ML1b. To be open while engineering these moves would be counterproductive as the inequities would be fully exposed to all.

The grade structure inherited from ML2 is reformed at ML3 for two reasons. Firstly, the delayered organisational structure requires fewer grades to span the hierarchy. Secondly, the metrics created under the PMS (see chapter six) enable fine differentiation of *individual* performance. Rewards are modified to reflect this, so, for instance, the fewer grades have broadband salary ranges.

The firm still benchmarks with the labour market, but in a more nuanced manner than at ML2. In order to remain competitive, the firm benchmarks by job family. So, scare human capital is less likely to be lost to competitors. Further, we saw in chapter five when discussing C&T that the enterprise identifies its rising stars and proactively implements calibre actions to retain and develop such talent. Thus, the firm may benchmark its rising stars against a different pay position in the relevant market. For instance, most employees may be benchmarked with the median in the market while rising stars may be linked to the upper quartile.

We saw in chapter six that one of the themes at ML3 is 'management by consequence'. Reward is one of those possible consequences. Individual performance is closely tracked and appraised through RRAA, IAR and ICR (see chapter six). Then, the individual's effectiveness is rated. A typical rating scheme is set out in Table 41. This illustrates a seven-point scale; some organisations prefer a five-point scale, in which case the three central ratings collapse into one; others prefer four- or three-point scales. The effectiveness ratings may use a forced distribution or a less severe expected distribution. The individual's rating is used to determine rewards (see below).

Table 41. Measure of Effectiveness		
Code	*Rating*	*Definition*
A	Outstanding Performance	An excellent performance Most objectives deliver excellent results All targets are met, many being stretching in nature Overall, an outstanding delivery to the organisation
B	Exceptional Performance	Performance consistently exceeds expectations Some objectives deliver excellent results All targets are met, with some being stretching All performance standards are met and many exceeded Overall, a significant delivery to the organisation
C+	Valued Performance (Plus)	A good level of performance where all targets are met and some exceeded All performance standards are also met and some exceeded Overall, a good delivery to the organisation
C	Valued Performance	A good level of performance where the individual delivers all key targets Performance meets the expected standards Delivery is suitable
C-	Valued Performance (Minus)	A good level of performance where most targets are met Other targets are close to being met All accountabilities are fulfilled satisfactorily Delivery is adequate
NI	Needs Improvement	Performance falls short of expectations Some targets are met but other key accountabilities are not fulfilled Some performance standards are not met Overall delivery needs to improve
US	Unsatisfactory	A clearly unacceptable performance Few targets are achieved Core accountabilities are not adequately fulfilled Performance standards are not in general met Significant improvements are essential

With the measure of effectiveness, salary reviews can now take into account the cost of living *and* individual delivery. Cost of living and company performance tend to set the pay budget. The distribution of that budget then depends upon *individual* performance. An example payout matrix is set out in Table 42. The fact that the potential payouts are expressed as a range reflects the fact that managers are granted some degree of discretion at ML3. This was absent at ML2. During the pay review process at ML3, managers are asked to make their pay award recommendation for each member of their team. Where they make a high or low recommendation, they are asked to add an explanatory narrative. Senior executives and HR reserve the right to override such recommendations where they seem out of place.

Table 42. Salary Review Payout Matrix				
Comp ratio (CR)*		*Below 90%*	*90–110%*	*Over 110%*
Annual Contribution Rating	A	6–8%	5–6%	3.5–4.5%
	B	3–4%	2.5–3%	2–2.5%
	C	1.5–3%	1.5–2.0%	1.0–2.0%
	NI	0–1.0%	0–1.0%	0–1.0%
	US	0%	0%	0%

*Comp ratio (CR) is the actual salary divided by the benchmark salary for the grade, expressed as a percentage.

STIP takes on a different form at ML3. The abundance of KPIs and the ability to differentiate performance on an individual basis means that bonus payouts can now reflect *individual* performance in the review year. The more sophisticated PMS, with monthly tracking and recording, reduces the danger of inequity that differential payouts would have had at ML2 and do have at ML1.

The *bonus pool* may still be linked to the overall profit performance of the business. The actual *bonus distribution* depends upon individual contribution to that profit performance. As at ML3, the organisation oscillates between decentralisation and centralisation, so the choice of profit alternates between SBU and total company profit.

The 'shape' of the STIP payout curve may still be a straight-line relationship, as discussed under ML2. However, the organisation may want to make a stronger statement that 'performance counts', so it may adopt a skewed distribution curve. This may resemble a Pareto power distribution – that is, few payouts at the lower end, most below the mean, and a long tail of ever-increasing payouts at the upper end. This reflects the expectations and evidence (see O'Boyle and Aguinis) that: few employees fail outright;

most deliver to expectation by hitting target, which is what they are paid a salary for; a handful perform exceptionally; and even fewer outstandingly. Bonus payouts reflect these exceptionals, proving that 'performance counts'. An example of a 'Pareto' payout curve is set out in Table 43.

Table 43. Short-Term Incentive Plan (STIP) Matrix			
Result vs. Target	100%		
Bonus Pool*	20%		
Performance Rating:	Bonus Multiple	Actual Payout*	Estimated Population
Outstanding plus	3.00	60%	3%
Outstanding	2.00	40%	12%
Valued Plus	1.50	30%	15%
Valued	0.80	18%	40%
Acceptable	0.40	8%	20%
Unsatisfactory	0	0%	10%

* as a percentage of salary.

It can be seen that the bonus rating levels are very similar to the salary review ratings. This reflects the tendency at ML3 to overemphasise 'performance' and essentially to 'double count' it through both salary rises and bonus payouts.

The company establishes a comprehensive recognition scheme at ML3 to reinforce the message of management by consequence (see Table 30). This is generally modelled on the needs of the non-bonusable population. In fact, certain grades or groups of staff may be officially or unofficially excluded from the scheme, e.g. sales staff on SIB and managers on STIP, in order to minimise the chances of rewarding the same achievement twice. Behaviours that are deemed to support the ethos of the business are recognised. The outline of a recognition scheme is set out in Table 44 as an example. Submissions for recognition awards are sent to a recognition review panel made up of senior managers. The panel meets monthly to decide the level of award to be granted based on the submission and the award level definitions.

The employee handbook and contract of employment evolve into, what we call, an 'employee portfolio'. This is a volume that contains all the

Table 44. Recognition Scheme

Award Level Criterion		'Standard'	'Bronze'	'Silver'	'Gold'
Definition		For doing a good job or deed within the responsibilities and expectations of the role	Extra effort, endeavour or achievement within the responsibilities and expectations of the role Going the extra mile	Significant effort, endeavour or achievement beyond the responsibilities and expectations of the role Value to stakeholders	Fanatical effort, endeavour or achievement and well beyond the role Significant and visible value to stakeholders
Accountability	Takes personal responsibility and demonstrates initiative, determination and persistence towards work	Does a good job or deed within the responsibilities of own role	Goes the extra mile by applying extra effort or endeavour within the responsibilities of own role, achieving a good result	Achieves value for the business by applying significant effort or endeavour beyond the responsibilities of own role	Achieves significant value for stakeholders by going well beyond the responsibilities of own role
Customer Focus	Understands and anticipates the needs of customers Passionately delivers service	Provides good and notable service for the customer within the responsibilities of own role	Goes the extra mile to achieve good service for the customer within the responsibilities of own role	Achieves value for the customer by applying significant service beyond the responsibilities of own role	Achieves significant and visible value for the customer by applying fanatical service well beyond the responsibilities of own role

Innovation	Initiates new ways of accomplishing results Creates business solutions and applies knowledge and insight to improve processes and results	Submits suggestion concerning current process and task in own work area with the intent of improving cycle time and/or reduced costs to a modest extent	Submits and implements a new solution to a problem in own work area that moderately improves efficiency and/or costs	Submits and implements a radically new solution in own work area or a new solution outside own work area that adds significant value	Submits and implements a totally novel solution outside own work area that adds substantial value
Target Value of Award	£10	£10	£50	£100	£500
Acknowledgement		HR letter	Manager letter	Director letter Article in Newsletter	CEO letter Photo in Newsletter
Message		"Thank you"	"Many thanks"	"Well done"	"Bravo"
Authority		Any employee can nominate Manager authorises	Any employee can nominate Manager approves award Senior manager authorises	Any employee can nominate Manager approves award Director authorises award	Any employee can nominate Manager approves award Director and HR Director recommend award CEO authorises award

documentation that defines the relationship between the employee and the employer: contract of employment; contractual entitlements; non-contractual entitlements; recognition awards; history of the company; key players' biographies; career structures; organisation charts etc. Held in a ring binder or a similar folder, this is a living portfolio with regular updates incorporated into it. At ML2, the contract tends to be merely the documentation handed to the employee prior to or soon after engagement. It is, at ML2, a static, historical piece of paper.

Every year, the company adds to the employee portfolio by issuing a total reward statement. After a few years' service, most employees forget the range of benefits that they are entitled to. The annual statement reminds them of this range and of its value.

ML4 – Integrated People Strategy

As we will see more clearly in the next chapter, the organisation moves to a 'total reward model' at ML4.

The employment deal that the company offers its workforce is explicitly defined – that is, what it offers in terms of career, personal development, pay, benefits, engagement etc. The deal is designed to tap into the full range of motivations (see chapter 10), hence the title of 'total reward model'. Thus, the reward manager is no longer confined to 'pay and rations', but takes an overview of all potential motivational factors. The ideal and logical model at ML4 is that of single status.

The company continues to benchmark with the market. However, it reverts to comparisons with one segment. As groups of the workforce that do not represent the firm's core competences have been outsourced, the enterprise's employees are now more homogenous. Further, the single status nature of the employment deal at ML4 would be undermined by differential benchmarking.

Salary is not just linked to performance, but also takes into account the strategic competencies introduced under C&T (see chapter five). These competencies are proven to enhance the potential for future performance, so pay is regarded as an investment in that future. Thus, the reward model moves from performance-related pay to contribution-related pay. Salary scales continue to be reviewed, as at lower maturity levels, on an annual basis.

Jobs are fairly narrow at ML2, with limited scope for individual flair.

Hence, salary bands are narrow, to the point that some jobs with virtually no discretion may have a spot salary for all workers in that job. Jobs evolve fully into roles by ML4. There is greater scope for individual aptitude and thus for differentiation. Employees can therefore be at different 'career stages' at the same level in the organisation. A model of such career stages is set out in Table 45. For some grades, this mirrors the skills matrix we discussed in chapter eight. Career stage is matched by pay position. As the employee develops in the role, demonstrates greater competency and contributes more and more at that level, the business endeavours to match salary commensurately. Recognition of such career progression may be addressed at the annual pay review. Managers at ML4 have much more discretion over rewards than they did at ML2. This is partially because all managers now work to a common set of 'what good looks like', i.e. the strategic competency framework.

Table 45. Salary Career Positioning Matrix			
Pay Level	*Definition*	*Salary**	*CR†*
'Entrant'	Contributing at the basic level for the role. A new appointment to the role and to this grade Competent at the basic level for the role Experience of the duties, processes and responsibilities of the role and level is still relatively low and new Not yet fully qualified and/or trained for the role Needs regular guidance from others for role tasks and processes	Well Below Midpoint	70 – 85%
'Developing'	Contributes to an acceptable standard Competent in all the core tasks, processes and accountabilities of the role Has moderate experience of most of the duties, processes, areas and responsibilities of the role and level Part or recently qualified in and/or trained for the role Needs limited support to fulfil the requirements of the role and level	Below Midpoint	80 – 95%

'Fully Qualified'	Contributes to the full requirements of the role and level Fully competent and skilled in all the core tasks, processes and accountabilities of the role Has full experience of all the duties, processes, areas and responsibilities of the role and level Fully qualified in and/or trained for the role Needs no support from others to fulfil the requirements of the role other than relevant supervision or review of results	Around Midpoint	95 – 110%
'Advanced'	Contributes well above the full requirements of the role and level Commands all accountabilities of the role and demonstrates superior skill and competency Has extensive experience of all the duties, processes, areas and responsibilities of the role and level Fully qualified and demonstrates CPD appropriate to the role and level Needs no support from others to fulfil the requirements of the role other than relevant supervision or review of results	Above Midpoint	110 – 125%
'Expert'	Exceptional contribution Commands all accountabilities of the role and demonstrates superior skill and competency Recognised as a role model and expert in own field Has extensive and intensive experience of all the duties, processes, areas and responsibilities of the role and level Fully qualified and demonstrates extensive CPD appropriate to the role and level Provides support and guidance to others	Well Above Midpoint	120 – 130%

* Salary level as position in salary band

† CompaRatio (illustrative per cent)

All now participate in the profit-related pay scheme (PRP). This reverts to a flat payment for all employees, thus favouring lower-paid workers. Long-term incentive plans (LTIP), which were reserved for executives at lower levels of maturity, are now open to all, through employee stock option plans (ESOP).

The reward strategy takes on a more logical feel at ML4. As part of this approach, the firm adopts reward product positioning. Here, each reward element takes on a unique position and purpose. Just as a company's effective product positioning ensures that it has one unique offering in each of its chosen market segments, so a reward manager positions each reward product. For instance, it is not uncommon for performance to be rewarded by both a salary rise and a bonus payment at ML2 and especially at ML3. This is inefficient and also confusing for internal players – the 'messages in the money' are ambiguous. Hence, at ML4 salary is repositioned to be linked with calibre (see chapter five) and PRP to be linked to performance in the period, usually the year. Hence, each reward product has an underlying unique reward position.

Benefits are offered on a cafeteria basis – a flexible benefit scheme. Each employee has a 'flex fund', which she can spend as she sees fit on the benefits offered through the scheme. Alternatively, the flex fund may be taken in cash. There may be a limit to the degree to which an employee may opt out of some benefits. For instance, where holidays can be traded, there may be a minimum threshold number of days' holiday, set either by the company or by statute, below which the individual may not trade.

Finally, the recognition scheme is adapted to reflect the values that have been established as guiding principles at this maturity level. All employees are eligible to participate.

Summary

The HR practices of R&R are summarised in Table 46. At ML1a, there are a limited number of R&R practices. The firm does not expand on this range at ML1b. Money is the central, if not the only practice. In fact, money is seen as the solution to most, if not all HR problems. Practices are ad hoc so a strong feeling of inequity pervades the business.

The organisation brings a rigid sense of order to R&R practices at ML2. This is a key theme from ML2a onwards, across the entire enterprise and all units. Job evaluation, job families and grading structures etc. reduce unfairness by establishing vertical and horizontal parity. The range of bonuses and benefits increases over that offered at ML1.

The core theme of performance and continuous improvement are supported by R&R practices at ML3. Pay becomes individualised at this level and the overriding message is that 'performance counts'.

Finally, at ML4, the firm shifts to a total reward model. Rewards are used to support the development of strategic competencies and thus the progression of the vision and values. The enterprise establishes an internally consistent and externally coherent employee value proposition (EVP).

We will cover the broader motivational agenda in the next chapter.

Table 46. Summary – Reward & Recognition			
ML	*OML*	*HRML*	

1	Entrepreneurial Management	Initial	a) Basic salary
			    Statutory benefits only
			    Basic payroll administration
			    Compliance with external and
			    internal regulations
			    Equity stake for founding team
			b) No unified, coherent reward
			    structure
			    Expedient offers, payments and
			    awards
			    Mixed 'messages in the money'
			    Money as a solution to all
			    problems
			    R&R for 'heroics'

2	Process Management	Foundational	Organisation-wide unified reward structure Horizontal, vertical and external parity Job families Job evaluation and sizing Grading structure Market benchmarking Pay policy positioning Terms & conditions matrix No local management discretion over rewards PCF Rewards as an annual event Cost-of-living pay awards

			STIP profit-related Hard formula SIP/SIB link Overtime pay LSA Benefits Employee handbook Contract of employment
3	Proficiency Management	HR Agenda	Comprehensible and transparent reward structure Broadbanding Individual pay differentiation based on performance MoE rating Individual salary payout matrix STIP award matrix: individual performance-related Moderate local managerial discretion Calibre-differentiated rewards Theme of 'performance counts' 'Double-counting' of salary rises and bonus payouts Comprehensive recognition scheme Employee portfolio Annual total reward statements
4	Systematic Management	Integrated People Strategy	Total reward model EVP Employment deal Contribution-related pay Salary career positioning matrix: CRP review Horizontal, vertical, external and personal equity PRP bonuses for all ESOP Reward product positioning Flexible benefits scheme Recognition scheme aligned to company values

CHAPTER 10

EMPLOYEE MOTIVATION

Introduction

In this chapter, we extend the discussion in the last chapter beyond the traditional compensation & benefits arena to the broader domain of motivation. We will see how a range of motivations exists, but that different motivations are enabled at different maturity levels. Further, the work practices and the HR practices at each individual maturity level actually hinder some motivations.

For ease of explanation, we have chosen to use the motivational framework as set out in Warr (2007). This is a comprehensive and a well-researched framework. For clarity, where a motivation is described in this chapter that is derived from Warr, it is printed in italics. The full list of motivations in this model is set out in the summary Table 47 at the end of this chapter.

ML1 – Initial

As we have seen, there are two contrasting phases at ML1. In the start-up phase (ML1a), motivation will be mixed. There will be the enthusiasm of being in at the start and creating something new. There will be the identification with the implicit or explicit mission of the new enterprise. Some will enjoy the apparent chaos; others will leave because of it. However, the type of motivations that will be accessible will almost entirely depend upon the style of the founder and the implicit blueprint she works by (see Table 3). Consequently, no common pattern can be described purely based upon maturity.

At ML1b, a pattern emerges. As we saw when discussing R&R (see chapter nine), organisations at this level are almost exclusively focused on extrinsic motivation. *Money* is regarded as the solution to all problems. In essence, money is the only solution systematically available to management at this level. Money is seen as the main reason people come to work. Thus, the psychological contract is transactional and short-term in nature. This is reinforced by the sense of job insecurity characteristic of ML1b. Ambiguity tends to be high and hygiene factors are generally neglected by management. Relative deprivation arises due to the inequities in management and reward practices.

Depending upon the nature of the work processes and/or production methodology, there may be some modest opportunity for *contact with others*. We will see that this grows as the organisation develops through the maturity levels.

Other employee motivations are available, but for the privileged few only. Job status – or *valued social positions* – is open to a few. *Opportunities for personal control* are available for a few senior players who benefit from the 'irresponsible autonomy' typical of ML1b. However, the heightened job and environmental ambiguity for most will crowd out chances for self-determination.

Thus, the 'motivational messages' are greatly mixed and confused. This leads to a greater problem in retention as staff leave due to the inequities. Demotivation results. Overall, motivation remains strongly extrinsic, but with multiple problems due to perceived inequities and unfairness.

ML2 – Foundational

Several EMs become accessible at ML2.

The appraisal procedure under PMS (see chapter six) provides the chance for *externally generated goals* for managers and sales staff. SMART goals and Management by Objectives (MbO) support this EM. The goals will tend to be motivational so long as they are optimal (neither too high nor too low), complete in nature and with minimal conflict with other goals and requirements.

The tightly defined jobs, the systematic use of job descriptions and the pervasiveness of SOPs give a degree of *role and environmental clarity* to employees. This reduces role ambiguity and anxiety. Three factors reduce this anxiety: standards of required performance; work method procedures; and work sequence scheduling. For business reasons, these are all spin-offs of fully implementing the work practices in ML2. However, the narrow job design will reduce *variety* and the opportunity for *personal control*.

Basic job training (BJT) and SOPs provide a limited opportunity for *skill use* and the demonstration of personal competency. Continued success at task completion raises employee aspiration levels.

Under EE (see chapter seven), we saw that health, safety and welfare needs were systematically addressed to manage hygiene factors. This gives an element of *physical security* to employees. In addition, through PMS, EE and R&R, just procedures and reward parity give an early sense of *equity*. However, we will see that this is not fully accessible until ML4.

Supervision at ML1b borders upon the abusive. At ML2, the BJT for managers, especially first line managers, provides a limited degree of *supportive supervisory environment* for employees.

ML3 – HR Agenda

More EMs become open and available at ML3.

The creation of functional career frameworks (see chapter five) provides *career opportunities* and progression for more employees than was apparent at ML2. This also enhances the awareness and probability of attaining *valued social positions* within the organisation.

Task variety is improved as jobs shift towards roles as the continuous improvement agenda progressively enlarges jobs. Similar to goals discussed above under ML2, there is an optimal level of variety. Too much or too little variety has a negative effect upon an individual's motivation and work happiness.

Goals are further enhanced at ML3 due to the appearance of KPIs, short-interval metrics and stretch CI targets. A fourth element in terms of *role clarity* adds to the three mentioned under ML2: regular feedback on actual performance. The monthly 1-2-1 meetings typical of ML3 enhances the opportunity for such feedback. However, the stretched nature of the goals reduces their optimality at ML3 and so may reduce their motivational effect.

ML4 – Integrated People Strategy

The organisation takes the final shift to a comprehensive intrinsic motivational framework through its total reward model (see chapter nine). We saw in chapter three that the business is able to fully articulate a vision and values that have proven to add value for the firm. This holds the integrated enterprise strategy together. Thus, the organisation can articulate the employment deal open to employees – perhaps defined as an employer brand or EVP. This guides HR and management practices.

The atmosphere of 'responsible autonomy' and the creation of the self-managed team (SMT) gives wide scope for *personal control* for most, if not all employees. The greater an individual's control over her environment, the greater her happiness – up to a point. Some studies suggest that high levels of autonomy can lead to anxiety over decision-making and overload. The expansion of the definition of roles in SMTs and the job enrichment associated with such structures further increase *variety*.

As we saw when discussing R&R (see chapter nine), vertical and horizontal equity (secured at ML2) are joined by personal *equity*, as procedural justice (addressed at ML2) is joined by distributive justice at ML4. Thus, with this scope for differentiation in terms of performance and competency, equity is not only achieved horizontally and vertically, as was established at ML2, but also personally. What each employee 'brings to the party' is reflected in his individual package.

Summary

In this chapter, we have seen how the practices at each maturity level both enable and hinder different motivations. Not all motivations are 'open' to every organisation at all ML. It is determined by the ML where the firm is located. The motivations are listed according to ML in Table 47. As can be seen, for example, expecting personal control to be relevant to all employees is only open at ML4. At any lower ML, this motivation will be available to only a privileged few. In essence, if the infrastructure of work practices associated with a given EM (and hence associated with the commensurate ML) is not in place, then that EM will not be systematically available to the firm located at that given ML. In other words, motivation is not a management choice, it is a dependent variable of the ML. This has broad implications for, and restrictions on the design of psychological contracts.

ML	OML	HRML	Employee Motivation

ML	OML	HRML	Employee Motivation
1	Entrepreneurial Management	Initial	*Money* *Contact with Others* Job ambiguity Environmental ambiguity Identification with founder's mission/blueprint Extrinsic Relative deprivation Insecurity Inequity
2	Process Management	Foundational	*Externally generated goals* for some *Environmental clarity* *Role clarity* *Security* Limited opportunity for *skill use* *Supportive supervision* *Equity* (horizontal and vertical) Low *variety* Limited *personal control* Hygiene factors
3	Proficiency Management	HR Agenda	*Valued social position* Task *variety* *Career opportunity and progression* Stretch goals may demotivate
4	Systematic Management	Integrated People Strategy	*Opportunity for personal control* *Equity* (horizontal, vertical and personal)

Table 47. Summary – Motivations by Maturity Level

CHAPTER 11

HUMAN RESOURCE STRATEGIC PLANNING

Introduction

In this chapter, we will take the debate to the next level – how to use the HRMM in order to devise an HR action plan. We will explain how to diagnose the current state of both the host business and the HR function. We will discuss how to conduct a gap analysis and craft a plan, including some classic priorities that must be accommodated. We end the discussion with how to market the HR plan internally and then manage it. We will see, as with all things, that the approach will differ according to the actual OML the HR practitioner faces at any one time.

'Quadrifocal' Strategic Vision

In the previous ten chapters, we have mapped out the strategic territory for all organisations and particularly from an HR angle. Now, we will consider how to navigate across that territory. We would recommend always having four 'horizons' in mind, hence the title of this section.

The ultimate goal is that of Human Resource maturity level 4 (HRML4). However, this is – for most HR functions and organisations – highly aspirational. It is a measure of 'world class' and the only viable state, but will remain out of the reach of most businesses. It would only be relevant for any one HR function if the client organisation was at OML4 currently or was about to venture on an improvement plan to move from OML3 to OML4. So, this will always be the aspirational horizon.

The long-term horizon will be the current maturity level plus one – that is, an improvement plan to shift to the next higher ML. We have seen that to even consolidate at the current ML requires a lot of energy and resource. Hence, the long-term goal of ML+1 may not seem ambitious, but it is unlikely to be achieved in a short timescale.

The medium-term horizon is full alignment with the current OML. This will consist of a prioritised list of HR practices that require designing and then fully implementing in, say, the next 12–24 months. This is where the HR plan resides.

The short-term horizon is doing the day job. Ignoring the day job undermines the standing of the function and fails in its primary service delivery to the client business. In addition, the short term consists of project actions to fulfil the HR Plan and handling any crises that arise in HR and in the wider organisation.

HR Strategy Process

The strategy process we recommend is straightforward. The stages in this process are:

- Diagnose the current business state
- Diagnose the current state of HR
- Conduct a maturity level gap analysis
- Design the HR Plan
- Market the provisional HR Plan
- Secure resources to deliver the HR Plan
- Manage the HR Plan
- Implement the HR Plan.

We will now explore each one of these stages in sequence.

Diagnose the Current Business State

Firstly, revisit the components of the organisational maturity levels that we encountered in chapter two. For ease of reference, we have duplicated the table from that chapter here (see Table 48). From observation of the organisation under study, provisionally categorise the OML of the business using Table 48 as a checklist. If the reader requires a more detailed checklist, she should refer back to Table 5. Note that to categorise the firm as, say, OML3, the work practices in question have to be fully institutionalised (see Table 49, which, again, is reproduced here for ease of reference). Where this is not fully the case, note the institutionalisation practice missing, e.g. policy in place, but no review process. Check all ML categorisations and validate them.

We should introduce a note of caution at this point. Business is influenced by fashion and the desire to adopt 'best practice' regardless of its efficacy.

There are, therefore, likely to be what we call 'misplaced artefacts' in all organisations. In chapter two, we referred to strategic plans at ML1 as fantasy documents. This is an example of a misplaced artefact, as 'strategic plans' only truly belong at ML4. Many organisations have defined and published their vision and values. However, as we have seen, these only have meaning at ML4. Also, when describing CI tools in chapter two, we explained that they only really come into their own at ML3, even though firms may adopt them at lower MLs. Thus, there may be examples in any subject organisation that are misplaced artefacts. In many cases, they will be policy statements only with no other institutionalisation practices to support them. In other cases, there may only be a coordinating role – an appointment of an employee with no resources to change or implement policy. The reader should be on the lookout for such misplaced artefacts. They can deceive the unwary who may take them as signals of a higher ML than the subject organisation warrants.

Table 48. Organisational Maturity Level – Characteristics
Organisational focus
Nature of organisational strategy
Open or closed system
The nature of work practices
The nature of project management
Organisational structure
Job design
Predominant management style
Predominant decision-making style
Organisational climate

Having gone through the elements of the OML, now determine the overall ML of the firm. Note that it is not possible for a firm to operate sustainably across more than one ML. If in doubt, the lowest common denominator (LCD) principle applies. For example, if there are some practices that appear to belong to ML3, but most belong firmly to ML2, the overall OML is likely to be level two.

Note also that it is feasible for different functions or units to operate at different maturity levels. This may be sustainable where there is limited interdependence and limited interaction between these functions or units. For example, in some businesses, marketing and transport have little to do with each other. However, where there is significant interdependence and interaction between functions or units at different maturity levels, a great deal of tension will arise. This will not be sustainable in the medium term.

Hence, note where different functions are at different maturity levels. This, in itself, may warrant some OE interventions.

Table 49. Institutional practices	
Policy statement	The organisational commitment to guiding principles and/or behaviours in a given practice area
Coordinating role	Role(s) with the assigned responsibility to coordinate activities at the organisational level Defines common procedures or assists units to define their own Reviews unit activities to ensure compliance Collects and shares experience across all units Provides advice as required The style of approach will differ according to the maturity level, e.g. advisory at ML2a
Funding and resources	Provision of funds, resources, materials, equipment, specialised skills and time to perform the activities
Skills to perform work practices	Provision of learning interventions to give the employees required to carry out the work practices the necessary specialised skills
Orientation to understand work practices	The provision of information to employees who need to know about the work practice These employees may be affected by the specific work practice in some way and thus require an understanding of the work practice
Documentation	Work practices are clearly defined and documented, covering some or all of the following: Policy statement (see above) Procedural steps Guidelines for managers Authority levels, roles and responsibilities Forms to progress procedures and authorise action
Plans to maintain work practice	The managerial commitment to create and follow a plan to implement and maintain the relevant work practices

Measurement	Metrics and other measurements to indicate: The extent of implementation of the work practices across the unit/organisation The effectiveness and/or efficiency of the work practices in any one unit to identify the need for corrective action and improvement
Verification of compliance to policy	The process assurance that work practices comply with policy and regulations, conducted by a person assigned that responsibility
Executive reviews	To provide insight to work practices at senior levels To provide overall governance of the policy and associated work practices

Diagnose the Current State of HR

In a similar vein, an analysis can be conducted to ascertain the ML of the HR function. As there is a fuller description of HR practices in this book, a more detailed analysis can be carried out for the HR function.

Take each HR pillar one at a time. For each pillar, note the HR practices that are actually used and fully in place. Note that for a practice to be in place, it must be fully institutionalised (see Table 49; Curtis et al, p.60-63). Where this is incomplete, note which institutionalisation practice is missing, e.g. policy in place but no metrics. Complete this exercise for each HR pillar.

Once complete, look across all HR pillars and determine the overall HRML. As with the wider organisation, the LCD principle applies.

Again, it is feasible for different pillars – that is, different HR sub-specialisms to be at different maturity levels. For instance, rewards and training may have little to do with each other. Again, HR in manufacturing and sales may have little to do with each other. However, where there is significant interdependency and integration between pillars or sub-specialism sections, tension will build. This will not be sustainable in the medium term.

Conduct a Maturity Level Gap Analysis

Now, simply compare the OML with the HRML. Note that the general principle is that the HRML should follow the OML. As a service function, HR should match its client organisation.

HRML may perfectly match the OML. This is unusual, but by no means impossible. Re-check the previous stages in the strategic process to validate your findings. If this match still exists, the probable underlying narrative in the company will be: HR is hand-in-glove with the organisation. If this is the case, you may move onto the medium-term plan.

If the HRML indicates that it is somehow ahead of the OML, then this is unusual. However, if this is the case, beware. If HR outpaces the client organisation, it can leave the function exposed. The probable implied narrative could be: HR over-complicates matters; HR is too expensive – an unnecessary luxury; they speak a foreign language; they talk down to us; they are intellectually arrogant.

The strategic options under these circumstance are as follows. Firstly, to encourage the organisation to 'catch up' with HR. However, HR could then be accused of arrogance and of interfering in work practices of other functions, which may be none of their business. Secondly, HR could consider treading water in the hope that the company would catch up with it. Hoping for this to occur without a plan and supporting resources is fanciful. Unless there is good prospect that other functions are likely to invest in such an improvement plan, HR will be waiting a long time. Then, the underlying narrative will simply get louder over time. Thirdly, HR could retrench to match the lower maturity level of the rest of the organisation. This is probably the most realistic option, however disheartening it may sound. The plan needs to build up practices that match the current OML and the carefully dismantling of the over-elaborate HR practices associated with the higher HRMLs. Remember, the overall principle here is to match the client organisation. It may seem like admitting defeat to retrench, but it is the sensible option in both the short and the long term.

Finally, the diagnostics may show that the HRML lags behind the OML. Experience would seem to show this is more often the case than not. The wider the gap, the greater the challenge and the greater the threat to the function. Possible current narratives could include: HR is holding back the business; HR does not step up to the plate; HR is out of touch; HR is not strategic; they are too transactional. Here, the previous stages of detailed diagnostics are critical. This helps to identify the key gaps, which can then feed the next stage in the HR strategy process.

Design the HR Plan

Whatever the gap analysis, there will be a need to close the gap, one way or another. The LCD principle applies here also – that is, the plan builds from the bottom up in each HR pillar. Lower maturity levels are the foundations for higher ones. If one ML is incomplete, attempting the implementation of practices of a higher level will be doomed. So, identify which pillar is the LCD. Identify practices at that ML and pillar that are yet to be put fully in place. Note them. Then, look across all pillars to ensure horizontal fit. Until all HR practices at the lowest level of maturity are in place, it is unwise for any pillar to advance to the next ML.

The list of actions may include two types. Firstly, the complete design and implementation of a brand new HR practice, one that is currently and completely absent from the business. Secondly, the design and implementation of one or more institutionalisation practice for an existing HR practice. This ensures the HR practice will eventually be fully embedded in the business.

The number of actions that can be completed in any one timeframe will be resource-constrained. However, there are some classic priorities that put them top of the list if they are currently absent. We will cover these in the next section.

Classic Priorities

Organisational effectiveness (OE) practices normally have to precede actions under any other pillar. Structures and tools need to be in place. More so with change management practices. All other actions in the HR Plan imply some form of organisational change. The level of sophistication of such change management practices needs to match the ML being built (see chapter four).

Compliance applies to all levels. In fact, if compliance is poorly maintained, it implies that the organisation, or at least the HR function, is trapped at ML1. In chapter two, we described the style of HR at ML1b as being 'legal, honest and decent'. If HR does not meet this standard, it is unlikely to succeed at all. HR, in essence, would lack integrity in such circumstances.

In earlier chapters, we commented on the dominant themes for HR at different maturity levels. These indicate an element of prioritisation if these themes are not supported at the target maturity level. Below, we repeat those themes.

At ML2a, there is an overriding need to have organisational-wide reward structures. If these are absent, inequities arise, organisational justice is undermined and all other practices will be hampered. HR will be engulfed with formal and informal grievances, and turnover will remain stubbornly high.

At ML2, systematic staffing and resourcing is a dominant theme. This is the principle way that HR practices can enhance organisational performance at this maturity level.

At ML3, performance management is the principal theme. Hence, HR has to put in the PMS tools to advance this theme. Further, it has to reform R&R practices to support the message that 'performance counts'.

At ML4, the vision and values in use are the prime theme. Note, these are derived from strategic competencies that have been proven to add value to the organisation and thus guide all other HR practices at ML4. Personal development as a theme then comes to the fore.

The HR Maturity Matrix – 'A Plan on a Page'

At this stage, there will be a long list of HR actions in priority order. These can be captured on one page of A4, as a visual guide to the strategic plan for HR. An example is sketched in Table 50.

Table 50. Human Resource Maturity Matrix – 'Plan on a Page'								
	OML	HRML	OE	C&T	PMS	EE	ED	R&R
ML4								
ML3	Proficiency Management		#5	#9	#6	#10	#8	#7
ML2		Foundational	#1		#2	#4	#3	
ML1								

In this example, the overall OML has been identified as OML3 ('proficiency management'), but the HRML is only at ML2 ('foundational'). HR must match the organisation. This is a 'catch-up' strategy.

Note that all the actions at HRML2 have to be completed *before* any at ML3 are addressed. HRML2 acts as a foundation for HRML3.

When all actions at HRML2 are fully institutionalised and bedded in, then those at HRML3 can be enacted. Also note that the first action at HRML3 is under OE. This is the bridgehead to enable all other actions at that ML. Further, as performance management is a dominant theme at ML3, the next two priority actions are under PMS and then R&R.

Marketing the HR Plan

So far, much of the work done to build the plan could be completed behind closed doors in the HR department. Best practice may dictate involving key stakeholders, but before considering this at this stage or any earlier stage, the discussion in this section should be taken into account.

The HR Plan is in 'HR speak'. We encountered this problem back in chapter one. Thus, the HR Plan may need to be translated into 'business speak'. This will be unique to each business. Only the HR practitioner can judge what vocabulary, conversations, arguments, statistics or presentational format is most likely to win over any relevant audience. However, the work in this book offers some general guidance.

There are two general indicators of the language that is most pertinent at any one maturity level. Firstly, the business focus at any one ML is what is most likely to resonate with relevant audiences. So, for example, efficiency and stability are the focus at ML2. This can be factored into any marketing of the HR Plan. Secondly, the dominant role of HR at that ML indicates the appropriate language. In the example used just now, at ML2, this role is that of service provider. As such, projects to improve the efficiency of HR so that it provides a more responsive service may gain approval. In all cases, it is important to describe how any proposed plan solves the problems of the organisation, at the current OML.

We now turn to the concept of a 'plan'. It will be evident by now that the term 'strategy' is really only truly applicable at ML3 and above. In its conventional sense, strategy does not exist at ML1 and 2. Remember also that programme management does not appear until ML3. So, talking 'strategy' or even 'plan' below ML3 would mismatch with the audience. It would be evidence that HR does not 'speak business'. Hence, at ML1 and ML2, any projects should be presented as separate actions designed to fix specific issues. In essence there is no 'plan', nor could there be a plan below ML3. This also explains the proviso on including colleagues from outside of HR in earlier diagnostic stages. If the suspicion were that the organisation could be at OML1 or 2, it would be counterproductive to involve others in devising a 'plan', let alone a 'strategy'. However, supporting individual HR projects may still remain an option below ML3.

One further cautionary note, only use the term 'maturity' if it is genuinely understood in the business in its technical sense (see chapter two). No CEO wants to hear that her organisation is 'immature'. Find another term or simply avoid the word 'maturity' if the technical meaning is not part of the client organisation's vocabulary, especially below ML3.

Taking all of the above into consideration, whether it is a plan that needs marketing or individual projects, support is needed from key stakeholders. Here, it is important to be clear on who constitutes the decision-making unit (DMU). Not all parties in the DMU are equal, and the messages often need to be tailored to suit. A checklist of DMU parties is set out in Table 51. The mnemonic 'ASPIC' can be used to summarise these roles. Before venturing into a marketing phase, it is best to put names to each category of member and plan how to win them over.

Table 51. Types of Decision-Making Units (DMU)	
Authority	The person who has the ultimate right to commit the organisation to action in this domain
Sentinel	Those whose input must be sought and who may hold a formal or informal veto over any proposal Their views must be incorporated into the final proposal These members act as gatekeepers or guardians over certain spheres
Proposer	The person who has the right to submit a recommendation for action in a particular domain
Implementer	Those who would have to execute any agreed action once it is decided
Contributor	Those who have a right to be consulted and give input on a proposal The input does not have to be incorporated into the final proposal or decision

Managing and Implementing the HR Plan

In the previous section, we explored whether the HR Plan was overt (at ML3 and 4) or covert (at ML1 and 2). Having agreed the plan (or projects) with the relevant DMU, it now falls to the HR team to manage the plan. There are two aspects to this, project planning and governance. Both should follow the style appropriate to the current OML.

At ML1b, there is no need for any overall governance. It is absent elsewhere in the firm. To apply anything other than a 'legal, honest and decent' approach in HR would be to encumber it with a regime that would slow it down, especially in the eyes of managers from other departments.

At ML2a, the projects should be managed in the same protocols that the business unit or function has adopted. At ML2b, it would be the project management disciplines that the overall enterprise has identified as its one best (internal) practice.

Table 52. Institutionalisation Practices	
Policy statement	The organisational commitment to guiding principles and/or behaviours in a given practice area
Coordinating role	Role(s) with the assigned responsibility to coordinate activities at the organisational level Defines common procedures or assists units to define their own Reviews unit activities to ensure compliance Collects and shares experience across all units Provides advice as required The style of approach will differ according to the maturity level, e.g. advisory at ML2a
Funding and resources	Provision of funds, resources, materials, equipment, specialised skills and time to perform the activities
Skills to perform work practices	Provision of learning interventions to give the employees required to carry out the work practices the necessary specialised skills
Orientation to understand work practices	The provision of information to employees who need to know about the work practice These employees may be affected by the specific work practice in some way and thus require an understanding of the work practice
Documentation	Work practices are clearly defined and documented, covering some or all of the following: Policy statement (see above) Procedural steps Guidelines for managers Authority levels, roles and responsibilities Forms to progress procedures and authorise action
Plans to maintain work practice	The managerial commitment to create and follow a plan to implement and maintain the relevant work practices
Measurement	Metrics and other measurements to indicate: The extent of implementation of the work practices across the unit/organisation The effectiveness and/or efficiency of the work practices in any one unit to identify the need for corrective action and improvement
Verification of compliance to policy	The process assurance that work practices comply with policy and regulations, conducted by a person assigned that responsibility
Executive reviews	To provide insight into work practices at senior levels To provide overall governance of the policy and associated work practices

ML3 introduces an overall programme management approach. This is where a medium-term plan fits the culture explicitly. Hence, HR should have its own programme management board to oversee progress of the HR Plan. Support from the PMO can be sought.

Then, at ML4, a portfolio management approach is adopted, governed by the SMO. HR should align with this approach.

The content of any project or plan will be unique to a firm. However, for HR, there is a general template to guide design and implementation. This is the list of institutionalisation practices we first encountered in chapter two. We reproduce it again as a checklist in Table 52 (Curtis et al, p.60-63).

One last word on implementation, regardless of the maturity level: we have guided the reader to apply a high degree of precision in designing the HR plan. Experience suggests that implementation requires a fair degree of flexibility. When any plan hits reality, it is severely tested – not because its design is faulty, but because it is impossible to assess all the variables that determine success. Thus, *how* the plan is realised may require some flexibility, or for some allowable variations or contingencies to be built into the plan. The plan itself may be negotiable at some or all of its stages.

Summary

In this chapter, we have taken the discussion to the next level – how to use the HRMM to devise an HR action plan. We have followed the tenet that HR should match and pace the host organisation – that is, to match the current OML by implementing the commensurate HRML. Then, to pace at the speed of development of the host organisation. We have offered diagnostic tools and analytical tools to aid the practitioner in this planning task and exhorted the reader to build in flexibility and contingency to improve the probability of successful implementation.

CHAPTER 12

HUMAN RESOURCE OPERATING MODEL

Introduction

In this chapter, we will explore the shape and structure of the HR function. In the literature, this is often referred to as the HR operating model. In the last chapter, we explored how to devise the HR plan. In this chapter, we will discuss how HR should be positioned in terms of skills, structure, role etc. We will see that the optimal HR operating model is different at each maturity level. The pressure and demands upon HR vary according to the ML of the host organisation. Hence, HR's positioning shifts accordingly. We end in discussing how this requires a radical rethink of the dominant framework for the HR operating model – the 'Ulrich model'.

The Dimensions of the HR Operating Model

For each maturity level, we will remind the reader of the following characteristics of the organisation:

- Organisational focus
- Nature of organisational strategy
- Organisational structure
- Nature of work practices
- Status of project management.

We will then discuss the dimensions of the HR operating model that best complement the organisation at that specific ML in terms of:

- HR dominant themes
- HR workload
- HR skills required
- HR structure

- HR style
- HR's dominant organisational role.

We offer the HR operating model at each ML as archetypes. Structure, in particular, will depend upon a multitude of factors, only one of which is ML: the size of the business; the number and skill sets of employees; the geography; locations; the industry etc. will all influence the shape, style and structure of HR. However, each ML implies a unique, specific logic for all dimensions of the HR operating model.

ML1a – Initial

The focus of the firm is to launch and survive. There is no explicit strategy, per se. All employees report to the founder. Work practices are formed through a trial and error approach and so they vary from day to day.

There is no HR staff, so there is no HR operating model. The founder/CEO 'does' HR as part of her role. She may be supported in administration, which deals with the transactional side of the work.

ML1b – Initial

As we saw in chapter two, the business focus here is on consolidation and growth. The strategy is emergent, but not fully articulated as yet. Structure is ad hoc with no organising principle. Work practices are evolving with minimal codification. Project management is makeshift, so varies from one project to the next.

HR is introduced to the firm as a new specialist function. There are, however, no dominant themes as such. HR has to deal with anything and everything. The only professional guidance is to be 'legal, honest and decent'.

HR's workload is variable and volatile. The staff have to deal with whatever comes along. In common with the rest of the organisation, HR practices are ad hoc.

Being new, the resource level is very low when compared to the workload. This may be supplemented with external experts as needs be, e.g. employment lawyers.

The skills required are thus generalist. As the workload is unpredictable and the resource level low, it would be grossly premature to specialise at this ML.

The head of HR (we will adopt the convention of calling her VP, HR from here on in) reports on an ad hoc basis. Where this is explicit, it could be to the CEO, the COO or even the CFO.

The optimal structure is a small, centralised HR office. There will not be any organising principle. Even though it is centralised, given the weight and volatility of the workload, the team may be on the road quite a lot.

The style of HR is highly reactive. The predominant organisational role fulfilled is that of 'compliance police', 'regulation guardians' and 'firefighters'. In policing such an organisation, HR is guided by the principle of 'legal, honest and decent'. At times, this will be an uncomfortable role to fulfil.

ML2a – Foundational

The business focus shifts to operational efficiency and stability. There is no explicit business strategy. The organising principle is functional and the structure reflects this. There is one general manager, the CEO. The VP, HR logically reports to him.

At ML2a, general policies are devised at the organisational level. The specific functional work practices are then designed and codified at the unit level, hence SOPs are local. Project management is basic and the adopted processes will be local in nature.

As mentioned in preceding chapters, the dominant theme for HR at ML2a is systematic staffing and resourcing at the local level. At corporate level, there is the unified reward policies and organisational-level common reward practices.

The workload for HR differs from the corporate to the local level. Only general company policies are crafted centrally. Thus, a thin central staff will be needed to draft policies, act as coordinating roles and verify compliance to policy (see institutionalisation practices in chapter two). The central HR unit may seek external expert support to help in this regard.

HR practices are developed in full at local level. As we have seen, these are based upon the 'rights and rules' as they apply to employees. Most of this work is transactional and centres on the foundational HR practices (see Table 9). These tools and practices are of a basic nature so do not need in-depth expertise. In common with other departments, demand for HR services is not measured at this ML and hence the detail of the workload is not known. Further, local managers need to have access to HR services and apply the practices to suit their local needs.

Overall, the skills needed are generalist. Such generalists are embedded in the local units as the practices are designed and implemented locally at

ML2a. For example, trainers may be operators embedded in the units, acting as trainers on a part-time basis as and when needed. These would act rather like local operational subject matter experts rather than L&D professionals. The exception is the reward policies and practices. These rest in the centre as a resource for the whole organisation. Hence, the one full-time specialist in the whole function will be in C&B.

The HR structure is thus logically devolved. The VP, HR reports to the CEO. A small central policy unit supports the VP, HR, especially on R&R. Local HR Managers (HRM) report to local unit managers e.g. factory managers, functional heads or business unit managers. HR staff to deal with the transactional workload reports into each HRM.

The style of the function is responsive. As it builds up the range of HR policies and practices, and embeds them in the company, it renders its operations more and more efficient.

The prime role is thus 'service provider'. In addition, the role of 'change agent' is taken on. This role is applicable to all maturity levels. The sophistication of how this role is played varies across the maturity levels (see chapter four). Lastly, HR takes on the role of 'employee advocate'. As the policies and practices derive from the rights and rules, HR is there to enforce them. Line managers need frequent reminders of employees' rights.

ML2b – Foundational

The HR positioning at ML2b is very similar to that described for ML2a. The business focus is the same, as are all the other features of the organisation, with one exception. Work practices are now common across the entire organisation. This modifies some aspects of HR operating model.

In line with the rest of the firm, HR establishes common HR practices across the whole company. There is thus a need for organisation-wide coordination roles. At ML2b, this role now crafts the policy *and* the practice to enact that policy, and verifies compliance with policy and practice. Thus, the specialist skills needed are higher than at ML2a. However, the project list does not tend to be long even at ML2b. So, these roles can, in the main, be part-time. This need for emergent specialist skills represents the embryonic centres of excellence (CoE) that we will return to under ML3. Overall, though, the need is predominantly for generalists.

The common approach across the entire enterprise implies that reporting should become centralised. The VP, HR continues to report to the CEO. There is a larger, though still thin, central team to support the VP, HR on policies and practices. HRMs are still embedded in local units with their transactional staff, but they now logically report directly to the VP, HR. Practice owners are part-time, so each HRM may take up a specialism to develop policy etc. with the exception of rewards, which remains a full-time central role.

ML3 – HR Agenda

The business focus is continuous improvement (CI). SBUs and their functions now have explicit medium-term strategies. Each SBU is headed up by its own general manager. The structure is now delayered and work practices have been re-engineered to become lean. Project management has evolved into programme management in support of the SBU and functional strategies.

The dominant theme for HR at ML3 is performance management – 'expectations management' and 'management by consequence'.

In common with other functions, HR is awash with KPIs. As a service function, these tend to be variations on reliability, empathy, relevance and responsiveness. HR seeks best-in-class practices and regularly benchmarks with other organisations. HR's toolbox needs to be more sophisticated at this maturity level.

HR now requires experts to cover each of the HR pillars. The demands of HR necessitate the regular re-crafting and updating of all policies and practices. Thus, centres of excellence (CoE) become fully established at ML3. Further, as demand for HR services is now measured, the workload becomes more transparent and quantifiable. This enables a more confident prediction of the level of need for each specialist skill. The staffing of the different departments in HR is therefore less problematic than it was at lower maturity levels.

However, there is still a need to support the SBU GMs. As with other functions, the GMs often want 'their' HRM to hand, hence HRMs still tend to be embedded. As generalists, they report jointly to the VP, HR and their SBU GM. Transactional work is still done locally in support of the GM. In common with the enterprise strategy, the central HR strategy is still embryonic. Hence, in reality, HR policies and practices are adapted to suit the SBU and functional requirements. The HRMs are, in essence, proto-HRBPs. As embedded generalists, the HRMs still retain specialist responsibility for organisational design and change management. Central CoEs focus on reward & recognition, calibre & talent, employee engagement, employee development and performance management.

As such, the HR structure evolves into a matrix structure. The HR style at this level is active. The prime organisational role is that of 'advisor' – experts in people, people management and managing through organisation. HR still retains the role of 'change agent', but that of 'employee advocate' tends to take a back seat at this ML. The heavy emphasis on outpacing the competition and achieving high financial results and the theme of 'performance counts' discourage HR staff from frequently speaking up for employees. The HR Advisors are primarily advisors to management.

ML4 – Integrated People Strategy

The business focus moves onto viability. There is now an explicit enterprise strategy. The structure is flexible – what we have called a 'lattice structure'. The orientation is towards end-to-end business processes, each of which has a process owner, and which are world-class. The OSM champions portfolio management.

The dominant theme for HR at ML4 is the vision and values. These are derived from the strategic competencies that guide all other HR practices.

Managers are now more rounded and take on much of the responsibility for people management. Some of the management tasks that they assumed at lower maturity levels are now embedded in SMTs. However, high-level skills such as diagnostics, internal consultancy and systems design still rest with HR. Policies and practices may be standardised, but people problems rarely come in standardised packages. Transactional work also still needs to be carried out, even where there is a self-service model in place.

Each line manager still has his own assigned HRM. We can adopt the convention of calling this role an 'HR Business Partner' (HRBP) as it only belongs at ML4, which is the only truly *strategic* maturity level. So each manager at level III (see Table 4) has a named single point of contact (SPOC) in HR – her HRBP.

The centres of excellence (CoE) now contribute to the integrated enterprise strategy bringing their expertise to bear. Further, transactional work is centralised in an HR Shared Service (HRSS) centre. This relieves the HRBPs of back office work. However, we will qualify this point about the HRSS in the next section.

In common with the rest of the business, the structure flexes at ML4. For effective deployment of resource, all nominally report to the VP, HR. However, project teams and task forces etc. form and disband regularly, and HR staff are allocated as needed from time to time. This lattice structure is thus multifaceted.

The HR style is now proactive. The roles adopted at ML4 are that of 'strategic (people) partner', 'organisational conscience' and 'cultural guardian'.

HR operating model is summarised in Table 53. ML1a is not shown, as HR is absent as a specialist function at this maturity level.

Table 53. Summary – HR Operating Model					
	ML1b	*ML2a*	*ML2b*	*ML3*	*ML4*
Dominant themes	None 'Honest, legal and decent'	Staffing and resourcing Corporate R&R policies and practices	As ML2a	'Expectations management' 'Management by consequence'	Vision & values Strategic competencies
Workload	Unpredictable Variable Volatile	Unknown	As ML2a	Transparent Measured (KPIs)	Fully transparent
Skills	Generalist	Generalist SME in R&R	Generalist Policy leads as emergent SMEs	SMEs in R&R, EE, C&T, ED, PMS HRMs as emergent HRBPs	Devolved to the line HR diagnostics, consultancy and systems design
Structure	Ad hoc Small centralised office	Devolved Small corporate centre	Centralised corporate policies and procedures Embedded HRMs	Matrix CoEs Embedded HRMs	Flexible HRBP CoE HRSS
Style	Reactive	Responsive	As ML2a	Active	Proactive
Dominant roles	Compliance police Regulation guardian Firefighter	Service provider Change agent Employee advocate	As ML2a	Advisor Change agent	Strategic partner Organisational conscience Cultural guardian

Qualifying the 'Ulrich Model'

There are a number of general conclusions we can draw from the preceding analysis of the HR operating model and a few specific ones.

It is clear that the HR operating model is radically different at the different maturity levels. As with other elements of the HRMM, one cannot implement the full model in one go. The 'Ulrich model' is no exception.

HR has to reinvent itself at every turn. As we have described in the previous sections, the logical sequence to building up to the full 'Ulrich model' is as follows:

- Generalists introduced at ML1b
- R&R CoE implemented at ML2a
- Embryonic CoE for other pillars introduced at ML2b
- Fully established CoE at ML3
- Embryonic HRBP at ML3
- Fully established generalist HRBP at ML4
- HRSS introduced at ML4.

As can be seen, the need for HR generalists exists all the way up to and including ML4. Further, the full 'Ulrich model' cannot be implemented until ML4. This should not surprise us as the improvement path underlying the HRMM is in itself an organisational learning curve. No organisation can learn all lessons in one go. Endeavouring to implement the full 'Ulrich model' in one go is too disruptive for any business. The foundations have to be established first. This is not unique to HR. As we have indicated throughout this book, rushing towards 'world-class' is folly.

The evidence would seem to support the points made here. In practice, the implementation of the pure 'Ulrich model' has been far from smooth. The 'three stool' model is a much more complex route for employees and managers to access HR services than the traditional single HR office. The split between HRSS, CoE and HRBP simply confuses the internal customers. Managers and employees prefer a one-stop solution. Hence, the SPOC described above.

There is also a more fundamental issue with the whole 'Ulrich model'. What HR sometimes describes as 'routine' and 'tactical' are considered as 'complex' and 'strategic' by line managers. They want expert input. Further, people problems are the 'field intelligence' that informs HR. Without this input, HR cannot ground or justify *any* strategic contribution. Prematurely channelling HRMs towards a strategic HRBP, while simultaneously separating their direct and regular contact with employees by diverting enquiries and queries to an HRSS, cuts the HRM off from her field intelligence. This separates the HRBP from the very nuggets that inform their strategic input. It actually undermines the very role of HRBP.

Hence the need to qualify the establishment of any HRSS. Client contact needs to be retained at the coalface. The HRBP and her local HR team have to remain the SPOC for managers and employees within their area of responsibility. In this case, the HRSS should only relieve the HRBP of back office support work. Otherwise, the HRBP becomes an empty role. In practice, either the HRBP holds onto transactional work or the role is rendered redundant. HR would therefore be reduced to an administrative function, the very opposite of the rationale for creating the role of HRBP in the first place.

Summary

In this chapter, we have argued that the HR operating model varies according to organisational characteristics. These primarily depend upon the maturity level of the host business. So, as the organisational focus, strategy and structure change, so must the HR dominant role, skills, structure etc. Thus, one size (of HR function) can never fit all (firms). So, using the predominant model, the 'Ulrich model', as a template, we have shown that this can only be implemented successfully in stages as the enterprise moves through the four maturity levels. Hence, it is only at ML4 that the full Ulrich model could be implemented successfully. To put it another way, the full 'Ulrich model' is unsuitable for most firms – it being a special case, not a general one. That is, because most firms will *not* be at ML4, implementing the full 'Ulrich model' would be a strategic misfit and hence a strategic error. In essence, the shape of the HR function needs to be tailored to the host business and especially to its organisational maturity level.

CHAPTER 13

CONCLUSIONS

The Size of the Strategic Task

Throughout this book, we have described around 250 HR and HR-related work practices as we have built up the HRMM, chapter by chapter. This quantity is merely a small sample of the full range of possible practices. It is well beyond the scope of this book to set out *all* possible work practices.

Further, to fully embed any one HR practice in an organisation requires that each of the ten institutionalisation practices be implemented for that one HR work practice. Thus, this book implies that there are at least 2,500 discrete projects necessary to move from ML1 to ML4 for HR alone. The logic of maturity models contends that there are no shortcuts. The road to world-class is a long one. Not surprisingly, some businesses settle for less. However, the logic of maturity models asserts that settling for less than ML4 may have dire consequences for the survival of the firm in the long term.

'Best Fit' versus 'Best Practice'

In terms of strategic approach, the HR literature has two major competing models. 'Best fit' supports the argument that the HR configuration or bundle of policies and practices should fit the unique requirements of the host organisation. Any HR solution is therefore bespoke. Conversely, the 'best practice' approach maintains that there is an HR configuration that consistently leads to superior business performance across any or all sectors – this is sometimes termed the 'high-performance work system' (HPWS).

This book suggests that this is a false dichotomy; the HRMM contains *both*. The 'best practice' approach is essentially ML4. This is the world-class standard. However, as we have shown, for the vast majority of businesses there is no means of achieving this in one go. Only highly mature organisations can seriously plan to attain ML4. In fact, for most firms, 'best practice' would be a strategic misfit. It would be neither suitable nor sustainable; it would be a waste of resources. Best practice should be considered no more than aspirational for the majority of enterprises.

The 'best fit' approach is captured in the underlying logic of the HRMM that HR practices should match the current OML. Throughout this book, we have implied that the 'best fit' approach is the appropriate strategy for organisations in the short-to-medium term.

Failure to follow the above guidelines results in strategic errors. One such error is to foist overly complicated HR practices and operating models on a company that is not yet ready for them. Another is holding onto relatively primitive HR practices that lack sufficient sophistication for an advanced organisation.

Strategic Alignment Revisited

The literature tells us the obvious – HR must align with the business strategy, period. As we have seen, this is not as easy as might first appear for the reasons that we have explored throughout this book. The company's strategy may not be well articulated – it may even be absent. In such circumstances, there is no obvious guidance for the VP, HR on what to do. The default is often to adopt a motley collection of 'best practices'. Consequently, this collection may prove random when compared with the model set out in this book. We saw in the previous section that adopting a 'best practice' approach is a doomed tactic for the majority of firms. HR would still be speaking a foreign language, if not gibberish.

We argued early on in this book that there was a need for a universal translator. The HRMM is that universal translator and the lingua franca is maturity. OML is, in essence, a surrogate for organisational 'strategy'. Every company has work practices and thus can be measured in terms of maturity, even if there is no explicit strategy. There is a matching HRML for every OML. Hence, HR should match the OML of their client organisations. An explicit alignment with an articulated enterprise strategy is a special case confined to ML4. This suggests that HR may have been searching for the wrong Holy Grail all these years.

Defining every HR Strategy

We may now return to Mintzberg's description of strategy – the 5 Ps. We will use this to define in broad terms what any and every HR strategy should be. To reiterate, according to Mintzberg, strategy can be perspective, position, plan, pattern and/or ploy. Given the logic of the HR Maturity Model, we can use each of these terms to delineate each and every HR strategy.

Perspective is the core purpose of HR, namely:

- Raising people and organisational capability and performance, and
- Enhancing employee satisfaction, significance and balance, in order
- To facilitate the short-, medium- and long-term success of the organisation.

Position is the optimal positioning of the HR operating model in terms of style, structure and organisational role at the given HR maturity level to deliver the plan.

Plan is the next series of HR practices to be implemented in priority/time sequence to match the organisational maturity level of the organisation.

Pattern is the collection of HR practices in the HR maturity level that matches the current organisational maturity level. This pattern is the external fit with the organisational maturity level and the internal horizontal fit between each and every HR strategic pillar (see chapter one).

Ploy is the general rubric for HR to 'match and pace' the organisational maturity level. Some may wish this ploy to be bolder – to match, pace and *lead* the organisation towards world-class (ML4). This bolder approach would make HR truly *strategic*.

Thus, we conclude with a comprehensive definition of *every* HR strategy, for *all* possible firms at *all* possible stages of organisational development. We now leave the reader to consider her own unique approach to HR strategic planning. We hope that this book has assisted you in some small way and that, in the process, it may have cleared some of the fog that obscures this fascinating and important subject.

Good luck!

REFERENCES & NOTES

General

Where there are no references for a particular chapter, the reader is referred to the general texts below. The general texts are relevant to most, if not all, chapters.

The prime sources for the underlying models that have informed and inspired this book are:

Armstrong, M (2003) *Armstrong's Handbook of Human Resource Management Practice*, Kogan Page

Cameron, K S and Quinn, R E (2006) *Diagnosing and Changing Organizational Culture*, Jossey-Bass

Curtis, B, Hefley, W E and Miller, S A (2002) *The People Capability Maturity Model*, Addison Wesley

Flynn, S M (2014) *A Practical Guide to Crafting Your HR Strategy: The Nine Fundamental Employment Deals*, CreateSpace

Kearns, P (2010) *HR Strategy: Creating Business Strategy with Human Capital*, Butterworth Heinemann

Mintzberg, H (1989) *Mintzberg on Management*, Free Press

Verweire, K and Van den Berghe, L (eds.) (2004) *Integrated Performance Management: A Guide to Strategic Implementation*, Sage

Chapter 1 – Introduction

For the discussion on business strategy, see:

Hambrick, D C and Fredrickson, J W (2001) 'Are you sure you have a strategy?' *The Academy of Management Executive*, 15, 4, pp.48-59

Mintzberg, H (1987), 'The 5 Ps of Strategy', *Californian Management Review*, Fall

For the Viable Systems Model, see:

Beer, S (1998) *Diagnosing the System for Organizations*, Wiley

Chapter 2 – Organisational and Human Resource Maturity

For a fuller description and analysis of employment models for start-ups, see:

Baron, J N and Hannan, M T (2002) 'Organisational blueprints for success in high-tech start-ups: lessons from the Stanford project on emerging companies' *California management review*, Vol. 44, No. 3

For an analysis of how early employment models persist and fade, see:

Baron, J N and Burton M D (1999) 'Engineering bureaucracy: the genesis of formal policies, positions, and structures in high-technology firms' *Journal of Law, Economics, & Organisation*, Vol. 15, No. 1

For an exposition of different measures of organisational effectiveness, see:

Cameron, K S and Quinn, R E (2006), *Diagnosing and Changing Organisational Culture*, Jossey-Bass

For a fuller description of the management styles used in this volume, see:

Hay Group, *The Ins and Outs of Successful Leadership: Helping You to Be a More Effective Leader*

On strategy ducks, see:

Liedtka, J (2006) 'Is your strategy a duck?' *Journal of Business Strategy*, Vol. 27, No. 5, p. 32-37

For reference to fantasy document, see:

Perrow, C (1999) *Normal Accidents*, Princeton University Press

For an early description of phases of the organisational life cycle and crises inherent in each phase, see:

Greiner, L E (1998), 'Evolution and revolution as organisations grow', *Harvard Business Review*, May-June

For a description of the different types of organisational structures, e.g. U-form, see:

Wilson, J F and Thomson, A (2006) *The making of modern management: British management in historical perspective*, Oxford University Press

For a fuller explanation of horizontal and vertical specialisation, see:

Mintzberg, H (1989) *Deriving configurations*, in *Mintzberg on Management*, Free Press

For the seven levels of responsibility, see:
Clement, S D and Clement C R (2014) *It's All about Work, Organising your Company to Get Work Done*, Organisational Design Inc.
Jaques, E (2006) *Requisite Organisation*, Cason Hall

On the Office of Strategy Management, see:
Kaplan, R S and Norton, D P (2008) *The Execution Premium: Linking Strategy to Operations for Competitive Advantage*, Harvard Business School Press

For a definitive explanation of different organisational units, see:
Goold, M and Campbell, A (2002) *Designing Effective Organisations: How to Create Structured Networks*, Jossey-Bass

On managing the white space, see:
Rummler, G A and Bracke, A P (1995) *Improving Performance: How to Manage the White Space on the Organisation Chart*, Jossey-Bass

On the lattice structure, see:
Benko, C and Anderson, M (2010) *The Corporate Lattice: Achieving High Performance in the Changing World of Work*, Harvard Business School Press

On 'irresponsible autonomy', see:
Ackroyd, A and Thompson, P (1999) *Organisational Misbehaviour*, Sage

Chapter 3 – Human Resource Strategic Framework

For reference to the cognitive limits of the number of relationships, see:
Barrett, L, Dunbar R and Lycett J (2002) *Human Evolutionary Psychology*, Palgrave
For 'managing through organisations', see:
Collins, D (2000) *Management Fads and Buzzwords*, Routledge

For closeness of supervision see:
Perrow C (1993) *Complex Organisations*, McGraw-Hill

Chapter 4 – Organisational Effectiveness

For general texts on organisational design, see:
Goold, M and Campbell, A (2002) *Designing Effective Organisations: How to Create Structured Networks*, Jossey-Bass
Jaques, E (2006) *Requisite Organisation*, Cason Hall
Stanford, N (2007) *Guide to Organisation Design*, The Economist Press

For a broader discussion on job design and the difficulty of specifying job descriptions as detailed inventories of tasks, see:
Marsden, D (2014) *A theory of employment systems: micro-foundations of societal diversity*, Oxford University Press

On the meaningfulness of work, see:
Bailey, C and Madden, A (2016) 'What makes work meaningful – or meaningless', *MIT Sloan Management Review*

On change management and the transition curve, see:
Hayes, J (2002) *The Theory and Practice of Change Management*, Palgrave Macmillan

For liaison devices, see:
Mintzberg, H (1989) *Deriving configurations*, in *Mintzberg on Management*, Free Press

On job crafting, see:
Wrzesniewski, A and Dutton, J E (2001) 'Crafting a Job: Revisioning employees as active crafters of their work', *Academy of Management Review*, Vol. 26, No.2, p.179-201

Chapter 5 – Calibre & Talent

On competency models, see:
Spencer, L M and Spencer, S M (1993) *Competence at Work: Models of Superior Performance*, Wiley

Chapter 6 – Performance Management Systems

On visual management, see:

Liker, J K (2004) *The Toyota Way*, McGraw Hill

On accountability, see:

Bergsteiner, H (2012) *Accountability Theory meets Accountability Practice*, Emerald

For 'crowding out' and the distinction between goals for learning and those for performance, see:

Sijts, G and Latham, G P (2005) 'Learning versus performance goals: when should each be used?' *Academy of Management Executive*, Vol. 19, No.1, p.124-131

For the Balanced Scorecard, see:

Kaplan, R S and Norton, D P (1992) 'The balanced scorecard – measures that drive performance', *Harvard Business Review*, Jan-Feb, p.71-79

For reference to 'management by exception', see:

Wren, D A (1994) *The Evolution of Management Thought*, Wiley

On the expectations approach, see:

Machin, J L J (1980) *The Expectations Approach: Improving managerial communications and performance*, McGraw Hill

On SMART and stretch goals, see:

Sitkin, S B, See, K E, Miller, C C, Lawless, M W and Carton, A M (2011) 'The Paradox of Stretch Goals: Organisations in Pursuit of the seemingly impossible', *Academy of Management Review*, Vol. 36, No. 3, p.544-566

Chapter 7 – Employee Engagement

For the different patterns of employee relations, see:

Purcell, J (1981) *Good Industrial Relations*, The MacMillan Press

On job crafting, see:

Wrzesniewski, A and Dutton, J E (2001) 'Crafting a Job: Revisioning employees as active crafters of their work', *Academy of Management Review*, Vol. 26, N.2, p.179-201

On the 4 Ps agenda for team briefings, see:
CMI Checklist 081 (2010) *Team Briefing*, Chartered Management Institute

For communication richness, see:
Jablin, F M, Putnam, L L, Roberts, K H and Porter, L W (1987) *Handbook of Organizational Communications, Sage*

For discussion on the variety of employer brands and employee value propositions, see:
Flynn, S M (2014) *A Practical Guide to Crafting Your HR Strategy: The Nine Fundamental Employment Deals*, CreateSpace

Chapter 8 – Employee Development

On the learning organisation, see:
Senge, P (1990) *The Fifth Discipline: The Art & Practice of The Learning Organisation*, Doubleday

On 70:20:10 rule, see:
Rabin, R (2014) *Blended Learning for Leadership*, Centre for Creative Leadership

Chapter 9 – Reward & Recognition

Armstrong, M and Murlis, H (2007) *Reward Management: A Handbook of Remuneration Strategy and Practice*, Kogan Page
For support for skewed payout matrices, see research on performance *not* following the normal Gaussian distribution:
O'Boyle, E and Aguinis, H (2012) 'The best and the rest: revisiting the norm of normality of individual performance', *Personnel Psychology*, 65, p.79-119

For an analysis of employment deals and related total reward models, see:
Flynn, S M (2014) *A Practical Guide to Crafting Your HR Strategy: The Nine Fundamental Employment Deals*, CreateSpace

Chapter 10 – Employee Motivation

Warr, (2007) *Work, Happiness and Unhappiness*, Lawrence Erlbaum Associates

For the different motivations at ML1a, dependent upon the founder, see:
Baron, J N and Hannan, M T (2002), 'Organisational blueprints for success in high-tech start-ups: lessons from the Stanford project on emerging companies', *California Management Review*, Vol 44, Issue 3

Chapter 11 – Human Resource Strategic Planning

For institutionalisation practices, see:
Curtis, B, Hefley W E and Miller S A (2002) *The People Capability Maturity Model*, Addison Wesley

Chapter 12 – Human Resource Operational Model

On the HR operating model, see:
CIPD (2015) *Changing HR operating models: a collection of thought pieces*

On the Ulrich model, see:
Boroughs, A (2014) *Ulrich comes of age: what have 18 years of the Ulrich model done for HR?* Orion Partners
Lambert, A (2009) *The Effective Business Partner*, Corporate Research Forum
Ulrich, D (1998) 'A new mandate for human resources', *Harvard Business Review*, Jan-Feb, p.124-134

On the confusion over the distinction between 'strategic' and 'transactional' and on what managers and employees want from HR, see:
Hirst, W, Carter, A, Gifford, J, Strebler, M and Baldwin, S (2008) *What Customers want from HR*, Institute of Employment Studies

Chapter 13 – Conclusions

For a fuller discussion of 'best practice' vs. 'best fit', see:
Boxall, P and Purcell, J (2011) *Strategy and Human Resources*, Palgrave and MacMillan

Boxall, P, Purcell, J and Wright P (2007) *The Oxford Handbook of Human Resources*, Oxford University Press

Kepes, S and Delery, J E (2007) *HRM Systems and the Problem of Internal Fit* in Boxall et al (2007)

INDEX